Vegan Meal Prep

Plant-Based Diet Guide for a Healthy Permanent Fat Loss, Understanding Alkaline pH + Over 101 Whole Foods, Anti-Inflammatory Ready-To-Go Delicious Recipes Cookbook & 21-Day Meal Plan

Copyright © 2019
- Aqiyl Moore -
All rights reserved.

Table of Contents

Introduction **9**
Chapter 1: The Alkaline Diet & Principles Involved **12**
Chapter 2: Breakfast Options **21**
- Apple Cinnamon Quinoa 21
- Avocado Wrap 23
- Blueberry Spelt Pancake 24
- Buckwheat Crepes 26
- Chia Seed Fruit Overnight Pudding 27
- Easy Quinoa Porridge 28
- Foolproof Weight Loss Breakfast Oats 29
- Low-Carb Grain-Free Cereal 30
- Maple Millet Porridge 31
- Pepper Avocado Quinoa 33
- Pumpkin & Buckwheat Pancakes 34
- Quick & Easy Quinoa & Apple Breakfast 36
- Raisin Millet Breakfast Treat 37
- Red Apple Pancakes 39
- Spelt Porridge 40
- Sprouted Toast With Cherry Tomatoes & Avocado 41
- Super-Seed Spelt Pancakes 42
- Vanilla Quinoa Porridge - Chai-Infused 43
- Warming Blueberry Porridge 44

Chapter 3: Lunch **45**
- Instant Raw Sushi Roll-Ups 45
- Mushroom Wrap 47
- Raw Broccoli Pesto With Zucchini Noodles 48
- Savory Sweet Potato Brunch Bowl 50
- Scrambled Tofu 51

- Soba Pesto & Pine Nuts 52
- Spinach & Chickpeas With Lemons 53
- Spinach & Tomatoes - Mac & Cheese 54
- Veggie & Grain Medley 56

Soup 57
- Black Bean Chili 59
- Broccoli - Mint & Ginger Soup 61
- Carrot - Apple & Ginger Soup 63
- Cauliflower & Leek Soup 64
- Cheesy Pumpkin Broccoli Soup 66
- Curried Sweet Potato Soup 70
- Ginger & Asparagus Broth 71
- Gut-Soothing Soup 73
- Healthy Minestrone 75
- Lentil Turmeric Soup 76
- Potato & Chickpea Curry 78
- Thai Green Vegetable Curry 80
- Tomato & Black Bean Soup 82
- Tuscan Bean Soup 83
- Vegetable Soup 85

Salad Options 87
- Apple & Avocado Sesame Salad 87
- Avocado Salad 88
- Barley & Fresh Papaya Salad With Nuts - Lime & Chili 89
- Preparation Technique - The Barley: 89
- Brussel Sprouts & Almond Salad 91
- Chopped Veggie Salad & Quinoa 93
- Corn - Heirloom Cherry & Bean Salad 94
- Creamy Kale Salad With Tomato & Avocado 95
- Cucumber & Tempeh Salad 96
- Detox Super Salad 98

Healthy Side Salad 100

Jicama & Fennel Salad 101

Julienne Salad Of Parsnip - Apple & Celeriac 102

Kale Caesar Salad 104

Lentil & Beet Salad 105

Lentil Salad 107

Roasted Sweet Potato Salad 108

Savory Sweet Salad 110

Spanish Bean Salad 111

Spring Beluga Lentil & Beet Salad With Coriander Vinaigrette 113

Summer Salad With Mint & Lemon Dressing 115

Tomato & Avocado Salad 117

Zesty Alkaline Salad Brussels & Kale 118

Chapter 4: Delicious Beverages & Smoothies 120

Milk Options 120

   Strawberry Rose Almond Milk 120

   Turmeric Milk 122

   Walnut Milk 124

Tea Options 125

   Alkaline Detox Tea 125

   Turmeric 'Bulletproof' Tea 126

Other Delicious Options 127

   Banana Milkshake 127

   Calm Down Adrenal-Healing Juice 128

   Fat Flush Juice 129

   Green Fruit Juice 130

   Green Power Shake 131

   High-Potassium Juice 132

   Hypothyroidism Re-Balance Juice 133

   Kiwi & Strawberry Popsicles 134

   Non-Dairy Apple Parfait 135

    Soy Cucumber Shake 136

Smoothie Options 137

    Almond & Avocado Green Smoothie 137

    Banana Smoothie 138

    Banana - Berry Green Smoothie 139

    Banana - Cacao Smoothie 140

    Chili Chai Hot Chocolate 141

    Crunch Berry Smoothie 142

    Grape - Parsley & Lemonade Smoothie 143

    Grapefruit & Green Tea Smoothie 144

    Lime Avocado Smoothie 145

    Mango Express Smoothies 146

    Mint Chocolate Ice Cream Smoothie 147

    Pineapple Green Smoothie 148

    Raspberry & Tofu Smoothie 149

    Spicy Gazpacho Grab Smoothies 150

    Spinach-Powered Smoothie 152

    Wild Coconut Curry 153

Chapter 5: Snacks 154

Dips & Spreads 154

    Alfredo Pasta Sauce - Vegan 154

    Avocado Green Pea Spread 156

    Black Bean Hummus 157

Other Delicious Snacks 158

    Chocolate Chip Banana Bread 158

    Chocolate Mousse - Vegan 160

    Dried Orange Slices 161

    Almond Joy Energy Balls – No-Bake 162

    Fresh Cherries - Nuts & Cream 164

    Ginger Cookie Bites 165

    Pumpkin Bread - Gluten-Free 166

Quinoa & Hummus Wraps ... 167
Spiced Pear & Apple Crumble ... 168
Strawberry Sorbet ... 169
Stuffed Coconut Figs ... 170
Zucchini Muffins ... 171

Chapter 6: Dinner & Side Options ... 173

Broccoli Mushroom Rotini Casserole ... 173
Butternut Squash With Spelt Pasta & Broccoli ... 175
Chickpea Frittata ... 176
Crispy Cauliflower Buffalo Wings ... 177
Festive Holiday Slaw With Pomegranate - Salted Caramel Pecans & Starfruit ... 178
Garbanzo Zucchini Cakes ... 180
Ginger Creamed Pecans & Chopped Kale With Pomelo ... 181
Greens & Tomatoes With Sprouted Lentils ... 183
Onion & Bell Pepper Masala ... 185
Pad Thai & Zucchini Noodles ... 187
Plant-Based Dinner Burger ... 189
Quinoa Stuffed Spaghetti Squash ... 191
Quinoa With Asparagus - Beetroot - Avocado & Fresh Kelp ... 192
Raw Veggie Chard Wrap With Ancho Chili Dip ... 194
Spaghetti Squash Patties ... 196
Spinach & Rice Balls ... 198
Stir-Fry With Lime & Coconut Quinoa ... 200
Stuffed Sweet Potato ... 202
Sweet Potato Veggie Biryani ... 204
Tofu Chili Burger ... 206
Vegetable Pasta With Tomato-Pepper Sauce ... 207
Wild Mushrooms & Spelt Pasta ... 208
Delicious Sides ... 210
Baked Beans ... 210

Brussel Sprouts With Lemon & Pistachios 212
Cauliflower Fried Rice 213
Cauliflower Mashed Potatoes 215
Chickpea & Spinach Medley 216
Healthy Asparagus 217
Roasted Root Vegetables 218
Sesame Ginger & Shiitake Cauliflower Rice 219
Summertime Coleslaw 221

Tasty Bread Options 222
Gluten-Free Bread 222
Spelt Alkaline Biscuits 224
Spelt Bread 225
Vegan: Spicy Sriracha Buttermilk Biscuits 227

Chapter 7: 21-Day Meal Plan 229
Chapter 8: A Final Word 235
Conclusion 238

Introduction

Congratulations on purchasing *Vegan Meal Prep* and thank you for doing so.

In this book we will talk first about how important is understanding the principles of Alkalinity and why a Vegan diet is essential nowadays.
The first part will involve the social problems, obesity, and side effects that the consumption of junk food has on your body. Junk food is any food that has zero nutritional value, including soft drinks and salty or oily snacks. The more these foods are consumed, the less you consume the essential vitamins and nutrients needed by your body.

Increased obesity issues are brought forward with the overconsumption of sugar, fats, and empty calories in so many foods. You may also experience learning problems and loss of memory since junk food causes a sudden inflammation in the hippocampus in the brain.

According to the *American Journal of Clinical Nutrition*, men who favored animal protein over plant-based protein in their diet had a greater risk of death in a 20-year follow-up than men whose diet was more balanced in terms of their sources of protein.

Ways Animal Protein Can Damage Your Health

Risk of Cancer is Increased: As you ingest proteins, the body will receive a higher proportion of amino acids, which results in the body producing higher levels of the hormone-insulin-like growth factor-1 (IGF-1). It is, unfortunately, the stimulation of the hormone which stimulates the cancer cell growth.

You Receive Less Fiber: If you enjoy, dairy, fish, eggs, poultry, and other animal products, you will not receive any fiber. According to the Institute of Medicine, men should consume a minimum of 38 grams of fiber daily. However, the average male consumes only about 15 grams daily. It spans further than that according to the USDA since almost all of the American civilization (95%) don't receive adequate fiber.

Animal Protein & Phosphorus: Animal protein revolves around high levels of phosphorous. This can lead to cardiac issues, heart attacks, heart failure, and sudden death.

The Worst Foods for Your pH Balance

It's very unfortunate that you cannot enjoy the following foods because of the acid-forming elements found in your body. Frequent consumption of these foods can lead to chronic diseases such as diabetes or a heart attack.

- Fried food
- Prepackaged or processed foods
- Fatty cuts of beef
- Soda & Beer

Chapter 1: The Alkaline Diet & Principles Involved

Alkaline Blood and the role of pH

Your blood pH can fall out of the normal range if left untreated. The pH is a measurement of how alkaline or acidic a particular food item is. Your normal pH ranges from zero to 14, as shown below:

- Alkaline basic ranges from 7.1 to 14.0
- Neutral is in the range of 7.0
- Acidic ranges from zero to 0.0–6.0.

Many elements of the alkaline diet suggest that most individuals will closely observe the pH of his/her urine to ensure it's in a safe zone. Your stomach contains generous amounts of hydrochloric acid, which give it a pH of 2.0 to 3.5. This is highly acidic, but the acidity is essential to break down the food consumed. Typically, this only occurs if you suffer from specific diseases such as ketoacidosis (a diabetic issue) or starvation.

According to research, "the human blood is always slightly alkaline, with a pH of 7.36 to 7.44."

If you measure your saliva and urine pH first thing in the morning, you will discover that they are very different. Your urine was all yellow, and your saliva was green and in the normal range. The reason for this is your urine will excrete all acids, impurities, and any unwanted elements filtered from your body by your kidneys. The urine ranges will vary throughout different times of the day.

However, it's generally more acidic than of saliva. Your saliva pH is usually higher than urine because the excess acids are excreted into the urine. Your saliva is simply filtered from the secreted blood in your mouth, which is designed to enhance the digestion process.

Ideally, the morning urine level should be between 6.5 to 7.5. Thus the saliva pH is altered by food residue and other similar items. An ideal morning saliva pH should be between 7.0 to 7.5.

What About Alkaline Water?

Research has not produced a lot of overwhelming results referencing the claims of how the alkaline diet can benefit your overall health. However, there's some light shown.

In 2014, Diabetologia, a German journal, published a survey where 485 women were observed. The study concluded that the individuals who had the most acid-formed diet plans had a much higher risk of developing diabetes.

In 2008, the *American Journal of Clinical Nutrition* discovered the high intake of potassium-rich foods, including veggies and fruits suggested by the alkaline organization, may assist older individuals in maintaining his/her muscle mass as the aging process occurs. The 3-year clinical trial involved 384 women and men from the ages of 65 years and up.

Another research study in 2013 was published by *Osteoporosis International*, which involved women ranging from 18 to 79 years. There was a "small but significant" connection between the maintenance of your muscle mass and the alkaline diet plan.

According to defenders of the alkaline diet, it's much healthier to eat alkaline foods than acidic foods. You will be creating a more alkaline-body environment. Some dietitians suggest an 80/20 ratio of alkaline-to-acid foods. In that method of thinking, the acidic environment created by acid-producing foods can cause disease.

The alkaline-acid balance of your blood must be stabilized through the food consumed daily. Thus, it's essential to give your body a constant supply of calcium, magnesium, potassium, and sodium. Each of these relevant minerals helps to neutralize the acid wastes you accumulate when you consume starches, sugars, and proteins.

Benefits of Alkaline Water

Antioxidant: The water can aid in the neutralization of free radicals that can cause cellular damage.

Clean Water: There is a pre-filtration cartridge inside the ionizer that removes prevalent pollutants existing in your tap water.

Alkalizing: You will restore your pH balance by reducing the acidity levels in your body.

Mineral Rich: You will gain higher concentrations of alkaline minerals such as potassium and magnesium.

Detoxifying: You can improve your body's ability to absorb important nutrients.

Oxygen Rich: You will be increasing the amount of dissolved oxygen in your blood.

Cleansing: As you continue with the alkaline diet, you will be helping to flush out toxins and acidic waste which have accumulated in your body over time through colon-cleansing properties on the plan.

Even though there's no significant scientific research, the elements provided by alkaline water are still believed to sustain proposed health benefits. These include:

- Your skin health is improved and better hydrated. Your immune system is supported by anti-aging properties absorbed by the liquid antioxidants.
- You achieve weight loss.

Possible Side Effects

You may suffer from skin irritations or gastrointestinal issues. If your body stores too much alkalinity, you may also interrupt your body's normal alkalinity, which can lead to metabolic <u>alkalosis</u> that can produce the following symptoms:

- Suffer from hand tremors
- Experience a slight tingling in your extremities or face
- Muscles may start twitching
- Become easily confused
- Become nauseous
- Have bouts of vomiting

Keep in mind, these are just precautions and may not have the same results with each individual.

You may ask if it's okay to eat fruits? The answer is fairly simple. Be on the lookout for anything with the last three letters of "-ose." Fruits should be treated as a treat. You should try to steer clear of all sugar, whether it is glucose, sucrose, or fructose.

At the same time, fruits also contain phytonutrients, fiber, vitamins, and so much more. The sheer amount of sugar that you will consume from some of those fruit choices could mean that this is not a worthwhile trade-off. Look over the next list:

Special Alkalizing Fruit Options

Your internal system can become upset in an <u>acidic body</u> environment. Alkaline foods with a pH level of 8.0 or higher, help to neutralize your body fluids and remove unwanted acid. The following are recommended daily servings of fruit for you to enjoy.

Blueberries

Blueberries are loaded with antioxidants, which help prevent cancer and promote cardiovascular health. Incorporate the delicious berries into jams, baked into pies, and your chosen recipes.

Grapes

Grapes contain essential vitamins and nutrients, including B2, Vitamin K, and copper to safeguard your brain, heart, and muscles. Try freezing them for a quick and easy snack for your weight loss regimen.

Pears

The phytonutrients provided in pears can help relieve heart disease and <u>type 2 diabetes</u>. Use them raw, steamed, or baked. The nutrition lives when the skin is left on when serving.

Kiwi

Kiwis are a key element which acts as a conductor to physical wellness since kiwi is packed with 85% Vitamin C. Their exotic colors provide a vibrant complement for smoothies and salads.

Papaya

Enjoy a portion of papaya if you're watching your weight. These filling and low-fat fruits will help keep your cravings at bay, help eliminate body fat and leave you feeling refreshed.

Cantaloupe

The essential vitamins in cantaloupes and other melons help strengthen immunity, improve eyesight, and aid in cerebral development. Enjoy delicious cantaloupes frequently to help lower your <u>high blood pressure</u> and high sugar.

Mango

Tasty mangoes are one of the tastiest tropical fruits. Mangoes will boost your body with over 20 <u>vitamins and minerals</u> to provide you with shiny hair, radiant skin, and so much more. Serve mango in-season for that scrumptious candy-like taste sensation.

Watermelon

Watermelons are a tasty hydrating and cooling summertime treat. Help keep your heart in shape with its high lycopene content. If you want to drop a few pounds, consume a low-fat portion of watermelon to ease those snack time hunger pains.

Tangerines

Select a healthy, low-calorie snack by choosing from tangelos, mandarins, cuties (a type of mandarin), or tangerines. Each of these citrus fruits has high levels of vitamins, folate, flavonoids, and potassium. They are easily peeled, making them a convenient mess-free fruit to enjoy while on-the-go.

A Few Options

The array of foods will provide you with beverages, whole grains, and other natural products. You'll have many nutritious choices that are both high in alkalizing properties and delicious at the same time. Here is a cheat for items you can substitute while on the alkaline diet plan:

Best Option	Forget These
Herbal Tea	Coffee
Almond Milk	Creamer
Sparkling Water	Soda
Chestnuts or Almonds	Peanuts
cold-pressed olive oil	Margarine
Fresh herbs & spices	Condiments
Finely crushed skinless almonds	Flour
Sweet Potatoes	White Potatoes
Frozen fruit - no additives	Canned Fruit
Basmati or wild rice	White Rice
stevia	Sugar
Agar-Agar	Gelatin
Lentils	Navy beans
Firm tofu or Poultry	Red meat
Lemon juice & Baking Soda	Yeast

| Sprouted Grains | Yeast Bread |

Chapter 2: Breakfast Options

Apple Cinnamon Quinoa

Total Yields Provided: 2 Servings

Ingredient List:

- Rinsed quinoa (1 cup)
- Vanilla milk (3 cups)
- Vanilla (.5 tsp.)
- Cinnamon (1 tsp.)
- Allspice (.25 tsp.)
- Raisins (.5 cup)
- Chopped apple (1 medium)
- Blueberries (1 cup)

Preparation Technique:

1. Combine all of the fixings except for the blueberries.
2. Simmer for five minutes and add the apples.
3. Simmer for another five to seven minutes (low to medium) until the bulk of the liquid is absorbed.
4. Take the pan away from the burner. Toss in the berries. Sweeten to taste.

Avocado Wrap

Total Yields Provided: **1 Serving**

Ingredient List:
- Hass avocado (.5 of 1)
- (1) collard leaf bunch
- Basil (1 tsp.)
- Spinach (1 small handful)
- Chopped cilantro (1 tsp.)
- Red onion (.25 of 1)
- Tomato (1)
- Sea salt & pepper (as desired)

Preparation Technique:
1. Rinse the veggies and chop or dice.
2. Spread the mashed avocado onto the leaf.
3. Sprinkle with the salt, cilantro, basil, tomato, red onion, and pepper.
4. Arrange the spinach on top to your liking. Fold in half and devour.

Blueberry Spelt Pancake

Total Yields Provided: **1 Serving**

Ingredient List:
- Ground flaxseed (2 tbsp.)
- Grapeseed oil (1 tbsp.)
- Maple syrup (1 tbsp. + extra for topping)
- Almond milk - unsweetened & unflavored (1.25 cups)
- Vanilla extract (1 tsp.)
- Organic blueberries (1 cup)
- Apple cider vinegar (1 tbsp.)
- Spelt flour (1 cup)
- Bak. powder (1 tsp.)
- Fine sea salt (.5 tsp.)
- Bak. soda (.5 tsp.)

Preparation Technique:
1. Combine the oil, almond milk, maple syrup, vanilla, ground flaxseed, and vinegar in a large mixing cup. Stir well. Let it rest for at least five minutes for the mixture to thicken.
2. Sift the spelt flour, salt, baking soda, and baking powder. Mix well with all of the fixings; some lumps are okay.
3. Add the blueberries and stir again gently just to combine.
4. Heat a non-stick griddle to 325° Fahrenheit.
5. Don't add any fat or oil to the pan. Instead, use a small portion of melted vegan butter.

6. Scoop out .33 cup of batter to use for each pancake. Pour onto the hot griddle.
7. Cook until the edges look slightly dried and golden with bubbles in the center of each pancake.
8. Flip the pancakes and cook for another 30 seconds.
9. Serve with maple syrup and additional blueberries.

Buckwheat Crepes

Total Yields Provided: 4 Servings

Ingredient List:
- Coconut oil (as needed)
- Buckwheat groats (1 cup)
- 100% vanilla extract (1 tbsp.)
- Pure water (.75 cup)
- Chia seeds (1 tbsp.)

Preparation Technique:
1. Rinse the buckwheat thoroughly and add water to set.
2. When ready to prepare, rinse, and drain.
3. Add the fixings into a blender and process until smooth.
4. Prepare a skillet using the med-high temperature setting to warm the oil.
5. Scoop and empty a thin layer of batter into the pan. Swirl until the mixture spread out over the bottom.
6. Flip it over when you notice the top of the crepe is no longer liquid. Continue with the remainder of the batter.
7. When they're ready, enjoy with a portion of hemp seeds, sprouted nut butter, freshly squeezed lemon juice, or your choice of other garnishes.

Chia Seed Fruit Overnight Pudding

Total Yields Provided: 1 Serving

Ingredient List:
- Chia seeds (.25 cup)
- Almond milk (1.25 cups)
- Maple syrup (1 tbsp.)
- Vanilla (1 splash)
- Colorful fruits (to your liking)

Preparation Technique:
1. Soak the chia seeds, the superfood, in the milk.
2. When it's time to eat, stir it well and add the rest of the fixings as desired.

Easy Quinoa Porridge

Total Yields Provided: 1 Serving

Ingredient List:
- Quinoa flakes (.5 cup)
- Chia seeds (1 tbsp.)
- Coconut oil (1 tbsp.)
- Plant-based milk (.25 cup)
- Ground cinnamon (.25 cup)
- Stevia extract (.25 cup)

Preparation Technique:
1. Soak chia seeds with 3 tbsp. water for 10 minutes or the night before.
2. Add the quinoa flakes with 1.25 cups of water.
3. Microwave for 2.5 minutes or prepare on the stovetop.
4. Stir in the chia seeds, coconut oil, milk, cinnamon, and stevia until combined.
5. Top with hemp seeds, crushed walnuts, or your favorite toppings.

Foolproof Weight Loss Breakfast Oats

Total Yields Provided: 2 Servings

Ingredient List:

- Oats (1 cup + 1.5 cups)
- Quinoa (.5 cup)
- Coconut oil (2 dessert spoons)
- Coconut or almond milk (as desired)
- Cinnamon (1 tsp.)
- Almonds (Small handful)
- Psyllium husks (1 pinch per person)
- Filtered water (1 cup or as needed)

Preparation Technique:

1. Prepare the quinoa combining water and quinoa. Simmer until the 1 cup of water is absorbed. Once it is almost cooked, add the cup of oats with water (1.5 cups or as needed). Simmer until the oats are also softened
2. Mince the almonds. Toss into the pan.
3. Remove the quinoa and oats from the burner when done.
4. Stir in the cinnamon, husks, coconut oil, and coconut milk or almond milk if you prefer.
5. Serve with a splash of milk or sweetened with a touch of the rice malt syrup if needed.
6. Garnish with a spoonful of almond butter to go on top.

Low-Carb Grain-Free Cereal

Total Yields Provided: 1 Serving

Ingredient List:
- Raw almonds (2 tbsp.)
- Raw walnuts (2 tbsp.)
- Raw sunflower seeds (1 tbsp.)
- Raw pumpkin seeds (1 tbsp.)
- Raw hemp seeds (1 tbsp.)
- Green apple (1 small)
- Ground cinnamon (.25 tsp.)
- Celtic sea salt (1 pinch)
- *For Serving*: Unsweetened almond milk or your choice

Preparation Technique:
1. Core and dice the apple. Crush the walnuts and almonds. Shell the hemp seeds.
2. Combine the measured fixings into a blender.
3. Prepare until creamy the way you like it.

Maple Millet Porridge

Total Yields Provided: 1-2 Servings

Ingredient List:
- Millet (1 cup)
- Water (10 cups)
- Salt (1 pinch)
- Cinnamon (1 tbsp.)
- Maple syrup (.25 cup)

Preparation Technique:
1. Prepare a large pot with the water.
2. Boil and add the salt and millet.
3. Reduce the temperature setting.
4. Secure a top on the boiling pot.
5. Continue cooking slowly for approximately 15 minutes.
6. Stir in the cinnamon and continue cooking for another 20 minutes.
7. When ready, add the maple syrup and stir before serving.

MINI CHICKPEA FLOUR FRITTATAS

Total Yields Provided: 4 Servings

Ingredient List:

- finely diced **red bell pepper**
- fresh, frozen or canned **corn** – I used frozen
- finely diced **jalapeno**
- roughly chopped **baby kale or spinach** – I used baby kale
- **dried basil** – thyme or tarragon would be great too!
- **garlic powder**
- **mineral salt or black salt** (don't skimp on the salt) – black salt (aka, kala namak) will add the distinctive sulphur flavor eggs are known for
- freshly **cracked pepper**
- optionally, add **nutritional yeast** for an extra savory, cheesy flavor

Preparation Technique:

1. Mix the batter, add the veggies and mix again.
2. Using a 1/4 measuring cup, scoop the batter and fill each of the 12 holes in the muffin tin.
3. Bake for 30 – 35 minutes.
4. Pull from the oven, turn muffins out and let rest on a cooling rack.

Tip: If not using a non-stick muffin tin, lightly grease each muffin hole. If using a non-stick tin, you don't need to oil the tin as the frittatas will fall out when turned over. You may need to gently tap the tin on a hard surface to release them. I didn't use any oil for these.

Pepper Avocado Quinoa

Total Yields Provided: 1 Serving

Ingredient List:
- Water (2 cups)
- Quinoa (.5 cup)
- Avocado (.25 to .5 of 1)
- Red pepper (.5 of 1)
- Carrot (1)
- Extra virgin olive oil (.125 cup)
- Bragg's Liquid Amino (.125 cup)
- Cilantro (.125 cup)
- Coriander/Cumin & Oregano (as desired)

Preparation Technique:
1. Bring the water to boil. Stir in the quinoa and let it boil for approximately 20 minutes.
2. Extinguish the heat and let it sit with the lid on until the quinoa is totally expanded.
3. In a blender, combine the rest of the fixings (omit the avocado) with .25 cup of the water until it's smooth.
4. Pour this mixture over the quinoa.
5. Slice the avocado and serve.

Pumpkin & Buckwheat Pancakes

Total Yields Provided: Varies

Ingredient List:
- Buckwheat flour (1.5 cups)
- Sea salt (.5 tsp.)
- Baking powder (1 tsp.)
- Nutmeg (.25 tsp.)
- Allspice (.25 tsp.)
- Ginger (.5 tsp.)
- Cinnamon (.5 tsp.)
- Medium pumpkin or butternut squash (.5 of 1)
- Ground flax seeds (2 tbsp.)
- Brown rice syrup (2 tbsp.)
- Almond milk (2 cups)
- Coconut oil (2 tbsp.)

Preparation Technique:
1. Make the pumpkin puree. Use a sharp knife to peel and chop the pumpkin into .75-inch pieces. Steam for 15 minutes until softened. Blend in a portion of oil.
2. Whisk the baking powder, salt, flour, and spices in a mixing container.
3. In another container, whisk the pumpkin, rice malt syrup, flax, and almond milk.
4. Mix it all together. Let it rest for about ten minutes.
5. Prepare a large skillet (medium-low) and warm up the oil.
6. After it's reasonably hot, spoon a large scoop of the batter into the pan.

7. Cook until it's bubbly. Gently flip and continue cooking until browned and done. Continue the process, adding oil as needed for each batch.
8. Serve immediately with coconut yogurt, fruit, or your favorite toppings.

Quick & Easy Quinoa & Apple Breakfast

Total Yields Provided: 1 Serving

Ingredient List:
- Quinoa (.5 cup)
- Apple (1)
- Lemon (.5 of 1)
- Cinnamon (as desired)

Preparation Technique:
1. Prepare the quinoa according to the instructions on the package.
2. Grate the apple, add and cook for about 30 seconds.
3. Serve with a sprinkle of cinnamon and raisins to your liking.

Raisin Millet Breakfast Treat

Total Yields Provided: 2 Servings

Ingredient List:
- Millet (2 cups)
- Filtered water (4 cups)
- Organic raisins (.66 cup)
- Cinnamon (.5 tsp.)
- Alcohol-free vanilla (.5 tsp.)
- Unsweetened almond milk (3 cups)
- Stevia (6 drops)
- Agave syrup - optional (1 tsp.)

Ingredient List - Possible Toppings:
- Chopped walnuts
- Sunflower seeds
- Raspberries
- Hemp seeds - optional
- Fresh mint

Preparation Technique:
1. Prepare the millet in the water in a saucepan. Once boiling, toss in the raisins and lower the heat setting (low).
2. Place a lid on the pan.
3. Simmer until the water has evaporated (10-15 min.).
4. Turn off the burner and let it rest for about ten minutes.
5. Pour in the almond milk (2 cups), cinnamon, agave, and stevia.

6. Warm it up for about one minute until the milk is absorbed and it's hot. Your mixture will become creamier.
7. Secure a lid on the pan.
8. Prepare the toppings: Spoon portions into the open bowls and sprinkle as desired.
9. Serve with 1 cup of almond milk.

Red Apple Pancakes

Total Yields Provided: 1-2 Servings

Ingredient List:
- Flour (.5 cup)
- Cinnamon (.5 tsp.)
- 15gr Flax Seeds
- Almond milk (.33 cup)
- Red apples (2 grated)
- Cooking oil

Ingredient List - The Garnishes:
- Low-fat frozen yogurt
- Peeled kiwifruit
- Blueberries

Preparation Technique:
1. Whisk the flour with cinnamon. Mix with the milk and 3 spoons of Flax Seed until smooth.
2. Add oil into a skillet using the low setting.
3. Cut and toss in the apple. Spread them out and cook for two minutes. Make separate batches out of them.
4. Serve with a portion of Soy yogurt, kiwi, and blueberries.

Spelt Porridge

Total Yields Provided: 2 Servings

Ingredient List:
- Filtered water (2 cups)
- Thin flaked spelt (.66 cup)
- Cinnamon (as desired)
- Agave syrup or powdered stevia (as desired)
- Alcohol-free vanilla (.5 tsp.)
- Dried cherries or cranberries (4-6 tbsp.)
- *Also Needed*: Coconut oil

Ingredient List - The Toppings:
- Hazelnut - unsweetened almond - hemp or rice milk (1 cup)
- Fresh raspberries, seeds, hemp nuts, raw nuts, blackberries blueberries, or strawberries

Preparation Technique:
1. Combine the first six fixings (1st section).
2. Simmer for three to four minutes using the medium heat setting.
3. Pour into a serving dish with milk.
4. Sprinkle with the toppings of your choice.

Sprouted Toast With Cherry Tomatoes & Avocado

Total Yields Provided: 1 Serving

Ingredient List:
- Hemp oil
- Avocado
- Cherry tomatoes
- Himalayan sea salt
- Sprouted Ezekiel toast

Preparation Technique:
1. Enjoy this one to your liking.
2. Toast the bread and add a generous portion of the avocado.
3. Top it off with a drizzle of oil, cherry tomatoes, and sea salt.
4. Serve for a delicious breakfast any time.

Super-Seed Spelt Pancakes

Total Yields Provided: 3 Servings

Ingredient List:
- Pumpkin seeds (.25 cup)
- Sesame seeds (.25 cup)
- Buckwheat groats (1 cup)
- Flax seeds (.25 cup)
- Chia seeds (.5 cup)
- Cinnamon (1.5 tsp.)
- Bak. powder (.5 tsp.)
- Fine sea salt (.25 cup)
- Bak. soda (1 tsp.)
- Stevia extract (.5 cup)
- Plant-based milk (2 tbsp.)
- Coconut oil (1 tsp.)

Preparation Technique:
1. Grind the first five ingredients into flour for the recipe.
2. Store about one-quarter of the seed flour for another time.
3. Whisk two cups of the flour with the rest of the fixings (omit the oil).
4. Achieve the right texture by adding small amounts of milk.
5. Warm a pan with a spritz of oil.
6. Pour thin layers of pancakes and flip once bubbles appear on top.
7. Continue the process until the batter is gone.

Vanilla Quinoa Porridge - Chai-Infused

Total Yields Provided: 2 Servings

Ingredient List:
- Dry quinoa (1 cup)
- Water - pref. alkaline (2 cups)
- Ground ginger (1.5 tsp.) or Fresh root ginger (1-inch piece)
- Cinnamon (1 stick or .5 tsp.)
- Ground nutmeg (.5 tsp.)
- Coconut cream or milk (.5 cup)
- Lemon or Lime (skin grated (.5 of 1)
- Vanilla bean pod (1)
- Assorted nuts and seeds (half a handful or as desired)
- *Optional:* Coconut yogurt - Ground cloves or grated apple

Preparation Technique:
1. Do the Prep: Grate the lime or lemon and ginger (if using the root).
2. Cook the quinoa and drain. Prepare the cloves to a powder. Scrape out the vanilla pod.
3. In a saucepan, add the quinoa with the spices (nutmeg, ginger, cinnamon, and cloves).
4. Pour the coconut cream/milk and vanilla pod into the pan.
5. Grate in the apple and toss it in at the end.
6. Once it's hot, serve in a big bowl.
7. Sprinkle with extra ground cinnamon and grated lemon rind.
8. Toss in the chia seeds

Warming Blueberry Porridge

Total Yields Provided: 1 Serving

Ingredient List:
- Buckwheat groats (.25 cup)
- Chia seeds (1 tbsp.)
- Almonds (10)
- Unsweetened almond milk (.5 cup)
- Stevia (1 pinch)
- Ground cinnamon (.25 tsp.)
- Vanilla extract (.25 tsp.)
- Blueberries (5 or as desired)

Preparation Technique:
1. Overnight, soak the groats with .5 cup of water.
2. Soak the almonds and chia seeds and almonds overnight with 2 parts water to the seed mixture.
3. Rinse and drain the buckwheat. Add to the milk in a skillet.
4. Cook for 7 minutes until it's creamy.
5. Combine all of the fixings and enjoy with five fresh blueberries.

Chapter 3: Lunch

Instant Raw Sushi Roll-Ups

Total Yields Provided: 2 Servings (10-12 rolls)

Ingredient List:

- Chickpeas/garbanzos (.5 cup)
- Almonds (1 handful)
- Tahini (1 tbsp.)
- Cumin (1 pinch)
- Olive oil (as needed)
- Garlic (1 clove)
- Lemon juice (.5 of 1)
- Himalayan salt (1 pinch)

Ingredient List - The Roll-Ups

- Medium zucchini/courgette (2)
- Carrot (1)

- Cucumber (1)
- Avocado (1)
- Coriander/cilantro (1 small bunch)
- Capsicum - yellow or orange pepper (1)

Preparation Technique:
1. Peel and slice the avocado. Rinse and drain the beans. Slice the cucumber, capsicum, and carrots into matchsticks.
2. *Prepare the almond hummus.* Toss each of the fixings into a blender and mix until creamy smooth. Pour in a little more olive oil and lemon in equal proportions to achieve the consistency you prefer.
3. *Prepare the Roll-Ups:* Cut away the tips of the zucchini. Carefully, use a vegetable peeler to peel the zucchini into thin, long strips.
4. Lay each zucchini strip out and spread a thick layer of the hummus onto the strip.
5. Decorate with the matchsticks of avocado, veggies, and several pieces of coriander.
6. Sprinkle on the sesame seeds, roll up, and serve.

Mushroom Wrap

Total Yields Provided: 1 Serving

Ingredient List:
- Mushroom (1 large)
- Firm tofu cubes (your choice)
- Chard (1 small handful)
- Kale or spinach (few handfuls)
- Olive oil (splash)
- Turmeric (1 pinch)
- Nutritional yeast (.125 tsp.)
- Spelt tortilla (1)
- *For the Garnish:* Salsa or guacamole

Preparation Technique:
1. This one is very flexible. Just choose your amounts and enjoy.
2. Prep the fixings and toss the mushrooms, firm tofu cubes, chard, and kale or spinach all together with a spritz of olive oil.
3. Toss in a skillet and stir until cooked to half of the original volume.
4. Season the mixture with salt, pepper, turmeric, and nutritional yeast.
5. Serve in the tortilla with salsa or guacamole on the side.

Raw Broccoli Pesto With Zucchini Noodles

Total Yields Provided: 4 Servings

Ingredient List:
- Olive oil (.5 cup)
- Fresh basil leaves - firmly packed (2 cups)
- Fresh lemon juice (3 tbsp.)
- Raw broccoli florets (.5 of 1 medium head broccoli or 1 cup)
- Pine nuts or blanched slivered almonds or raw walnuts (.5 cup)
- White miso paste or chickpea miso for soy-free (2 tsp.)
- Minced garlic (2 tsp.)
- Celtic sea salt (.75 tsp. or to your liking)
- Freshly cracked black pepper (.25 tsp. or as desired)

Ingredient List - To Serve:
- Zucchinis (4 small or 2 large) spiralized to make zoodles
- Finely diced English cucumber (1 cup)
- Finely chopped raw broccoli florets (.5 of 1 medium head or about 1 cup)
- Shelled hemp seeds (.25 cup)

Preparation Technique:
1. Prepare the pesto. Pour the lemon juice, olive oil, basil, pine nuts, broccoli, miso or parmesan, pepper, garlic, and salt into your blender.
2. Process for 20 to 30 seconds or until mostly combined, but not completely smooth.
3. Use your hands to lightly toss the zucchini noodles with diced cucumber and broccoli in a large salad dish until well combined.

4. Gently massage one cup of the pesto through the zucchini noodles until evenly coated.
5. Add additional pesto gradually to your preference. As you massage, the fruits and vegetables will release water making the pesto easier to work with.
6. Season with salt and pepper as desired.
7. Set out four salad plates. Swirl equal portions onto plates and toss with hemp seeds.
8. Serve immediately with any remaining pesto at the table.
9. *Note:* If serving this recipe as a dip with raw veggies or crackers or on sandwiches or wraps, hold back on .5 tablespoon of lemon juice and .25 teaspoon of salt. Adjust to taste.

Savory Sweet Potato Brunch Bowl

Total Yields Provided: 1 Serving

Ingredient List:
- Olive oil (.5 tbsp.)
- Minced garlic (2 tsp. or about 2 cloves)
- Spinach (2 cups)
- Sweet potato puree (8-oz. can) or Mashed sweet potatoes (1 cup)
- Pumpkin seeds (3 tbsp.)
- Sesame seeds (2 tsp.)
- Black pepper and salt (as desired)

Preparation Technique:
1. Warm the oil using the medium heat setting in a stovetop skillet until glistening.
2. Mince and add the garlic. Sauté until fragrant (1 min.).
3. Fold in the spinach and sauté until wilted (1 min.).
4. Scoop the sweet potatoes into a bowl. (If you'd like them warmed, add to a small sauté pan and heat for 30 to 60 seconds using the medium temperature setting.
5. Top with spinach, sesame seeds, salt, pepper, and pumpkin seeds.
6. Serve.

Scrambled Tofu

Total Yields Provided: 1-2 Servings

Ingredient List:
- Onion (1)
- Cloves (3)
- Tomatoes (3)
- Firm tofu (as desired)
- Cumin (.5 tsp.)
- Paprika (.5 tsp.)
- Turmeric (.5 tsp.)
- Yeast (.5 cup)
- Baby spinach (as desired)
- Salt (to your liking)

Preparation Technique:
1. Dice the garlic and onion.
2. Toss the onions into a pan and sauté (7 min.).
3. Toss in the garlic. Sauté for one additional minute.
4. Fold in the tofu and tomatoes. Continue cooking for ten minutes.
5. Sprinkle in the cumin and paprika. Stir well and add water as needed.
6. Stir in the spinach at the end.

Soba Pesto & Pine Nuts

Total Yields Provided: 2 Servings

Ingredient List:
- Pine nuts (8.5 oz.)
- Soba noodles (1 pkg.)
- Cold-pressed olive or flax oil (1 cup)
- Basil - parsley & coriander (1 bunch of each or as desired)
- Himalayan crystal salt & Freshly cracked ground pepper (to taste)
- Optional: Extra steamed veggies - ex. zucchini, broccoli, peas, semi-dried tomatoes, etc.

Preparation Technique:
1. Prepare the noodles according to the instructions on the packet.
2. Toss and rinse the basil, coriander, and parsley. Blend with a small portion of the oil and the pine nuts.
3. Toss in the rest of the fixings. Blend until you have a creamy sauce.
4. Mix together with the pesto in a saucepan.
5. Dust with the pepper and salt before serving.

Spinach & Chickpeas With Lemons

Total Yields Provided: 2 Servings

Ingredient List:
- Extra-Virgin olive oil (3 tbsp.)
- Onion (1 large)
- Garlic (4 cloves)
- Grated ginger (1 tbsp.)
- Grape tomatoes (.5 of a 1-pint container)
- Lemon (1 large)
- Crushed red pepper flakes (1 tsp.)
- Chickpeas (1 large can or to your liking)
- Sea salt - Himalayan or Redmond Real Salt (to your liking)

Preparation Technique:
1. Pour the oil to a large skillet.
2. Rinse and drain the beans.
3. Thinly slice and toss in the onion. Sauté approximately five minutes or until it starts browning.
4. Zest and juice the lemon. Toss in the grated ginger, lemon zest, minced garlic, tomatoes, and red pepper flakes. Sauté for about three to four minutes.
5. Fold in the chickpeas. Cook for another three to four minutes. Add the spinach. When the spinach starts to wilt; spritz with the lemon juice and sea salt.
6. Simmer for another two minutes and serve.

Spinach & Tomatoes - Mac & Cheese

Total Yields Provided: 8-10 Servings

Ingredient List:
- Macaroni pasta (4 cups)
- Vegan spread (.33 cup)
- Plain flour (.33 cup)
- Plant milk (2 cups)
- Vegan cheese (1.5 cups)
- Cherry tomatoes (.5 cup)
- Spinach (Couple of handfuls)
- White onion (1 large)
- Optional: Nutritional yeast (2 tbsp.)
- Salt and pepper (as desired)
- Oil - Frying the onion

Preparation Technique:
1. Warm the oven in advance to 360° Fahrenheit.
2. Finely chop the onion.
3. Rinse the spinach. Wash and slice the tomatoes into halves.
4. Pour water into a pot and add to salt. Wait for it to boil.
5. Prepare the macaroni for 8 minutes on a low boil. Drain and rinse under the cold tap to prevent further cooking, set aside.
6. In a saucepan, melt your vegan spread.
7. Once melted, add in the flour to form a smooth paste.
8. Simmer for two minutes, whisking as you go.
9. Pour in small portions of the milk.

10. Heat gently and continue to whisk for after approximately three to five minutes.
11. Season with salt and pepper as desired after the sauce has thickened.
12. Grate and add 3/4 of the chosen cheese. Stir well until melted. Stir in the crème Fraiche.
13. Add and sauté the onions until crispy. Add into the cheese sauce, save a few to sprinkle on top.
14. Combine the spinach and pasta into the cheese sauce. Pour into a large ovenproof dish.
15. Scatter the halved cherry tomatoes, nutritional yeast, and remaining grated cheese over the top. Sprinkle with a dusting of pepper and a touch more salt.
16. Prepare in the heated oven for approximately 20 to 25 minutes.
17. Serve immediately while piping hot.

Veggie & Grain Medley

Total Yields Provided: 1 Serving

Ingredient List:
- Quinoa (.5 cup)
- Millet (.5 cup)
- Peas (.5 cup)
- Diced celery (.33 cup)
- Diced beets (.5 cup)
- Brussels sprouts (2 cups)
- Summer squash (.5 cup)
- Sweet potato (.5 cup)

Ingredient List - The Salad:
- Shredded lettuce
- Sunflower sprouts
- Grated carrot
- Slivered red onion
- Small avocado (1 sliced)

Preparation Technique:
1. Boil and simmer the quinoa and millet until softened according to the package instructions.
2. Prepare the steamer basket with the peas, celery, beets, sprouts, squash, and sweet potato.
3. Add the veggies and cooked grains in a bowl and combine.
4. Combine the salad fixings.
5. Prepare the salad and serve the veggie medley dish for a great combo!

Soup

Cream of broccoli and white beans from Spain

Total Yields Provided: Varies

Ingredient List:
- 1 large broccoli
- 1 leek
- 230 g boiled white beans of Spain
- 150 ml non-sweetened soy milk
- 1 clove of garlic
- Timo q.b
- Peel of 1 lemon
- Vegetable broth
- Salt and pepper

Preparation Technique:
1. Wash and finely slice the leek and lightly fry it in a large pan with a drizzle of oil, thyme and garlic clove. In the meantime, clean the broccoli, divide the tops into small pieces and cut the stem into cubes. Add it to the leek with the beans, salt and pepper, and let it cook for a few minutes. At this point remove the garlic clove, and pour enough soy milk and vegetable broth to cover the vegetables. Allow to simmer 15 minutes until the broccoli is soft but not completely broken.

2. With the immersion blender reduce everything into a smooth and homogeneous cream. If it turns out to be too thick, you can stretch it with a bit of vegetable broth or unsweetened soy milk. Put the cream on the heat enough time to boil again, then serve it, finishing each portion with a pinch of grated lemon peel.

Black Bean Chili

Total Yields Provided: 6 huge servings

Ingredient List:
- Large onion (1)
- Large carrots (2)
- Green bell pepper (1)
- Cooked black beans (6 cups)
- Organic crushed tomatoes (1 large can)
- Garlic cloves (2)
- Chili powder (2 tsp. or to your liking)
- Black pepper (2 tsp.)
- Vegetable broth or Olive oil (2 tbsp.)
- Salt (as desired)
- Smoked paprika (2 tsp.)
- Sweet potato chips
- Cilantro - chopped for garnish

Preparation Technique:
1. Prep the Veggies: Drain and rinse the beans. Chop the carrots, onions, seeded bell pepper, and cloves of garlic.
2. Warm up the broth/oil until hot in a large soup pot with a top.
3. Toss in the carrots, bell pepper, onion, and garlic. Simmer for three to five minutes.
4. Fold in the rest of the fixings. Leave the lid off and *gently* simmer for 30 minutes (low-med).

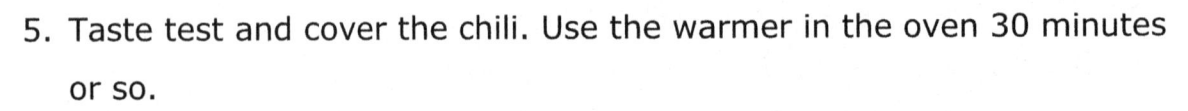

5. Taste test and cover the chili. Use the warmer in the oven 30 minutes or so.
6. Serve with a sprinkle of cilantro.

Broccoli - Mint & Ginger Soup

Total Yields Provided: 2 Servings

Ingredient List:

- Rough-crushed broccoli (1 large head or approx. 1.5 cups)
- Brown onion (1 small)
- Garlic (2 cloves)
- Fresh mint (.5 of 1 bunch)
- Cucumber (.5 of 1)
- Fresh root ginger (.5-inch grated)
- Organic vegetable stock (2 cups)
- Himalayan salt & Black pepper (as desired)
- Coconut or avocado oil (1 tbsp.)

Preparation Technique:

1. Mince the garlic and onion. Prepare a frying pan with oil and sauté for two to three minutes. Add the chopped broccoli.
2. Sauté for another one to two minutes.
3. Finely mince the ginger root and roughly chop the mint. Toss in and stir.
4. Pour in the stock to cover the broccoli, saving the remainder for blending to achieve the desired consistency.
5. Let this simmer for three to four minutes until the broccoli _just_ starts to soften.
6. Roughly chop the cucumber. Transfer everything to a blender, adding the spinach and raw cucumber. Blend using the high-speed setting until smooth.
7. Pour in additional stock to get the consistency you like.

8. Serve with a sprig of mint atop each bowl with a drizzle of avocado or olive oil.

Carrot - Apple & Ginger Soup

Total Yields Provided: 4-6 Servings

Ingredient List:

- Carrots (1 lb.)
- Apple (large)
- Vegetable broth - low-sodium preferred (4 cups)
- Raw cashews (.5 cup)
- Ginger root (1 tbsp.)
- Unsweetened almond milk (1 tbsp.)
- Fine sea salt (as desired)

Preparation Technique:

1. Soak the cashews covered with alkaline water for at least eight hours.
2. Drain the cashews when ready to prepare.
3. Pour in the almond milk and freshly grated ginger root into a food processor. Blend until smooth.
4. Peel, dice, and steam the carrots and apples until tender (5 min.).
5. Toss into a soup pot with the vegetable broth. Cool to room temperature.
6. Puree with an immersion blender until creamy.
7. Pour back into the soup pot. Stir in the cashew-ginger mixture with 2 tsp. of salt. Simmer, don't boil and serve while hot.

Cauliflower & Leek Soup

Total Yields Provided: 4-6 servings

Ingredient List:
- Grapeseed or olive oil (2 tbsp.)
- Minced garlic (2 cloves)
- Sliced leeks - white parts only or Diced yellow onion (2 cups)
- Celtic sea salt (1 tsp. or more as desired)
- Cauliflower (1 large head)
- Vegetable broth (7 cups)
- Blanched slivered almonds or raw unsalted cashews (.25 cup)
- *For Serving*: Chopped chives (3 tbsp.)

Preparation Technique:
1. Warm up the oil using the medium heat temperature setting.
2. Sauté the leeks, garlic, and .25 teaspoon of salt until the veggies are soft (3 min.).
3. Fold in the roughly chopped cauliflower. Continue to simmer for an additional minute.
4. Stir in the vegetable broth. Raise the temperature setting to high.
5. Once the water starts to bubble, lower the temperature setting to medium.
6. Let it simmer for about 20 to 30 minutes or until the cauliflower is tender.
7. Take the pan from the burner and wait for the soup to cool slightly.
8. Stir in the nuts.
9. Pour the soup into a blender in batches if needed. Pulse using the high setting until creamy smooth (1 min.)

10. Return the soup back into the saucepan using the low heat setting. Stir in salt as desired. Simmer.
11. Ladle the soup into serving bowls. Top it off with either chopped chives or grated nutmeg.

Cheesy Pumpkin Broccoli Soup

Total Yields Provided: 4 Servings

Ingredient List:
- Coconut oil (1 tbsp.)
- Onion (1 medium)
- Garlic cloves (2 minced)
- Chopped celery (1 cup)
- Broccoli florets (4 cups)
- Chopped pumpkin or butternut squash (3 cups)
- Vegetable broth (4 cups)
- Almond or other plant-based milk of your choice (depending on the thickness preference (2 cups)
- Nutritional yeast (4 tbsp.)
- Optional: Cayenne pepper or flakes (.25 tsp.)
- Lemon juice (.5 tbsp.)
- Pink salt & black pepper (as desired)
- Freshly chopped parsley (.25 cup + more for the garnish)
- *Optional:* Smoked paprika (As a garnish)

Preparation Technique:
1. Chop the onion and garlic. Melt the oil and cook until the onions are translucent (5 - 6 min).

2. Transfer the soup to the blender with the almond milk. Blend until smooth or a bit chunky; your choice. You can reheat the soup if you wish.
3. Stir in lemon juice, pink salt, and black pepper.
4. Garnish using the chopped parsley and smoked paprika.

Cream of Brussels sprouts with mustard and pomegranate

Total Yields Provided: Varies

Ingredient List:

- 450 g of Brussels sprouts + 20 sprouts to keep apart
- 400 g of potatoes
- 1 Tropea onion
- 1 l of vegetable broth extra virgin olive oil
- Salt to taste
- 1 teaspoon of delicate mustard
- 50 g of almond grain
- two tablespoons of pomegranate grains (optional)
- the bark of a biological orange
- 1 tablespoon of soy cream (to decorate)

Preparation Technique:

1. First clean the sprouts well by removing the toughest part and the outer leaves. Then divide them into quarters with a sharp knife. Now wash, peel and dice the potatoes and finally finely chop the Tropea onion.Simmer for 24 - 48 hours. Skim away the fat occasionally.
2. In a non-stick pan, quickly sauté the chopped onion with a drizzle of extra virgin olive oil, then add the potatoes, the sprouts and cook for 5 minutes. You can add a tablespoon of cooked broth to prevent the vegetables from sticking to the bottom of the pan. Now add all the vegetable broth, stir and continue to cook over moderate heat for about 25/30 minutes or until the potatoes and sprouts are very soft. With an immersion blender blend the vegetables until the desired creaminess is obtained, correct with salt and add the mustard.Trash the solid parts and strain the rest through a colander into a container.

3. Separately, clean the remaining sprouts and cut them in half. In a non-stick pan heat a drizzle of extra virgin olive oil and toss for a few minutes. They will have to be cooked but remain crunchy. Toasted in a non-stick pan the almond grain: will serve to give greater aroma to the dried fruit. Prepare to serve the soup in small bowls, decorating each one with the sautéed Brussels sprouts, the pomegranate grains, the orange peel and the chopped and toasted almonds.

Curried Sweet Potato Soup

Total Yields Provided: 4 Servings

Ingredient List:
- Coconut oil (1 tbsp.)
- Ginger (.5-inch chunk)
- Cloves of garlic (4)
- Lime (1)
- Curry (2 tsp.)
- Sweet potatoes (3)
- Full-fat coconut milk (15 oz. can)
- Filtered water (2 cups)
- Chopped cilantro (.5 of 1 bunch)

Preparation Technique:
1. Warm up the coconut oil in a large saucepan using the medium temperature setting.
2. Zest and juice the lime. Slice the potatoes into 1-inch pieces with the peel on or off.
3. Slice and crush the ginger and mince the garlic and lime zest. Cook for about three to four minutes.
4. Stir in the curry and simmer for about one minute.
5. Fold in the sweet potatoes, water, and coconut milk. Let the mixture boil. Lower the temperature setting to low and simmer for 25 minutes.
6. Place a lid on the cooker. Extinguish the heat and leave on the stovetop for about 30 minutes for the flavors to meld.
7. Prepare the soup in a blender.
8. Top it off with the cilantro and lime juice.

Ginger & Asparagus Broth

Total Yields Provided: 2 Servings

Ingredient List:
- Gluten-Free vegetable bouillon - ex. Marigold brand (3 cups)
- Filtered water (2 cups)
- Bragg Liquid Aminos or gluten-free tamari (1.5 tbsp.)
- Fresh ginger root (1-inch)
- Garlic cloves (2)
- Fresh red chilies (1)
- Asparagus (8 stalks)
- Kale (1 large handful)
- Spring onion (1)
- Fresh coriander (.5 cup)
- Olive oil (as needed)
- Coconut oil (2 tbsp.)
- Cracked black pepper (as desired)
- Himalayan salt (to your liking)

Preparation Technique:
1. Peel and grate the ginger. Chop the coriander, asparagus, kale, chili, and onion.
2. Use the medium heat setting to heat the filtered water, coconut oil, vegetable bouillon (stock), and Bragg Liquid Aminos or gluten-free tamari in a pan.

3. Stir in the chopped garlic, chili, and ginger.
4. Simmer for about 3 to 4 minutes.
5. Fold in the asparagus, kale, coriander, and spring onion. Simmer for another 3 to 4 minutes and serve.

Gut-Soothing Soup

Total Yields Provided: 4 Servings

Ingredient List:

- Lentils (15 oz. can)
- Sweet potato (1 large)
- Avocado (1)
- Spinach (1 large handful)
- Carrots (2)
- Bell pepper (1 red)
- Chopped dill (2 tbsp.)
- Cashews (1 handful chopped)
- Cloves of garlic (4)
- Brown onion (1)
- MSG-free - Yeast-free - vegetable stock (200ml./.85 cup approx.)
- Coconut oil (1 tbsp.)

Preparation Technique:

1. Rinse and drain the lentils. Set aside. Roughly chop and deseed the bell pepper.
2. Warm a saucepan with the oil. Roughly chop the garlic and onion.
3. Remove the peel and roughly chop the carrots and sweet potato. Toss into the pan with the oil. Sauté for about two minutes.
4. Pour in the vegetable stock to boil for 10 minutes until the vegetables are just warmed - not overcooked.
5. For the last five minutes, stir in the lentils.
6. Transfer to a food processor or blender.
7. Toss in the avocado, bell pepper, dill, and spinach.
8. Blend until smooth.

9. Garnish with a few dill sprigs, chopped cashews, and a spritz of oil.

Healthy Minestrone

Total Yields Provided: 2 servings

Ingredient List:
- Eggplant - aubergine (.5 cup)
- Sweet potato (.5 cup)
- Zucchini - courgette (.5 cup)
- Carrot (.5 cup)
- Red onion (.25 cup)
- Cloves of garlic (2)
- Beans - kidney, navy, etc. (.5 cup)
- Coconut oil (1 tbsp.)
- Vegetable stock (1 cup)
- Basil (1 handful)
- Tomato juice - fresh or bought (1 cup)
- Himalayan salt & black pepper (to your liking)

Preparation Technique:
1. Wash and cube the eggplant, potato, and zucchini. Dice the carrot and onion.
2. Prepare a large pot. Gently sauté the fixings in the coconut oil for about two minutes.
3. Stir in the beans, stock, and tomato juice. Once it's boiling, lower the temperature to simmer for 8 to 10 minutes.
4. Sprinkle with the basil and serve. Season how you like it.

Lentil Turmeric Soup

Total Yields Provided: 4 servings

Ingredient List:

- Pumpkin (200 grams - approximately .875 or 7/8 cup)
- Carrots (4)
- Sweet red potato (1)
- Tomatoes (4)
- Garlic (3 cloves)
- Mustard seeds (1 tsp.)
- Red onion (1)
- Vegetable stock (1.25 cups)
- Coconut cream (200 ml or .85 cup)
- Fresh coriander/cilantro (1 handful)
- Fresh turmeric root (1-inch)
- Red pepper (.5 of 1)
- Fresh ginger root (1-inch)
- Lentils (1 cup)
- Coconut oil (as needed)

Ingredient List - Optional Toppings:

- Cashews (.5 cup)
- Pumpkin seeds (2 tbsp.)
- Clove of garlic (1 minced)
- Thinly sliced red chili

Preparation Technique:

1. Chop the tomatoes, red onion, coriander/cilantro, garlic, peeled ginger, and turmeric - roughly peeled).
2. Heat a portion of the coconut oil in a pan. Toss in the onion and sauté one minute. Stir in the mustard seeds, ginger, turmeric, and garlic.
3. Stir in the root veggies (pumpkin, carrot, and sweet potato), tomatoes and red pepper. Coat the veggies in the oil.
4. Pour in the lentils and stock. Lower the temperature setting to simmer until the veggies soften and the lentils cook.
5. Once everything has softened, fold in the coconut cream and chopped cilantro. Empty into a blender and mix until smooth.
6. Prepare the optional topping. Mash the cashews on a chopping board. Cook with the pumpkin seeds and coconut oil with the minced garlic.
7. Serve the soup in bowls with, a drizzle of coconut cream, a sprig of cilantro, and the cashew topping with optional chili.
8. *Note*: If you're using dried lentils, you will need to add an additional .25 cup of the stock (allowing an additional 10 mins cooking time).

Potato & Chickpea Curry

Total Yields Provided: 8 Servings

Ingredient List:
- Olive oil - for cooking
- Sweet potatoes (4 medium)
- Diced tomatoes (1 can)
- Cooked chickpeas (1 cup)
- Onion (1)
- Chili pepper (.5 of 1 or to taste)
- Cumin seeds (1 tsp.)
- Large garlic cloves (3)
- Turmeric powder (1 tsp.)
- Salt (.5 tsp.)
- Garam masala (1 tsp.)
- Bay leaves (3)
- Yellow mustard seeds (1 tsp.)
- Full-fat coconut milk (1 can)
- Fresh spring onions for garnishing

Preparation Technique:
1. Finely chop the pepper. Heat a large pan using the medium heat temperature setting. Pour in a portion of olive oil. Toss in the cumin and mustard seeds after the pan is hot. Fry the spices for 3 to 4 minutes or so.
2. Dice the onion and toss into the pan.

3. Finely chop the garlic and add to the pan. Sauté for about five minutes.
4. Pour in the canned tomatoes. Stir in the remainder of the spices – whole bay leaves, chopped chili pepper, garam masala, turmeric, and salt. Sauté for three minutes.
5. Peel the skin from the potatoes and dice into bite-size chunks. Toss into the pan. Stir well until they're evenly coated with the tomatoes.
6. Lastly, pour in the coconut milk. Cook for approximately 15 minutes.
7. Fold in the chickpeas. Stir well and simmer for an additional 18 to 20 minutes. The potatoes will be fork-tender when ready.
8. Extinguish the heat source. Let the curry to stay in the pan for about ten more minutes to thicken up.
9. Top it off with a serving of fresh spring onions.

Thai Green Vegetable Curry

Total Yields Provided: 6 Servings

Ingredient List:
- Gluten-free vegetable stock (2 cups)
- Thai green curry paste (2-3 tsp.)
- Small sweet potato (1)
- Broccoli (1 head)
- Small eggplant (1)
- Medium-sized zucchini (1)
- Red bell pepper (1)
- Coconut milk (1-2 cups)
- Kaffir lime leaves (2-3)
- Fresh ginger, grated (1-2-inches knob)
- Juice (1 lime)
- Coconut aminos (2-3 tbsp.)
- Salt and pepper (as desired)
- Whole grain jasmine rice for serving

Preparation Technique:
1. Prepare a large pot with the vegetable stock. Wait for it to boil.
2. Toss in the chopped vegetables, kaffir lime leaves, grated ginger, and enough coconut milk to cover the vegetables. Let it simmer, covered, for 20-30 minutes, stirring occasionally.
3. Dust with salt and pepper. Simmer covered until the veggies are fully cooked (5-10 min.).

4. Take the pot from the heat. Add the lime juice and coconut aminos. Stir to combine. Serve with some whole grain jasmine rice.

Tomato & Black Bean Soup

Total Yields Provided: 4-6 Servings

Ingredient List:
- Tomatoes (6-8)
- Dry beans (2 lb.)
- Medium onions (2)
- Olive oil (.5 cup)
- Cloves of garlic (2)
- Oregano (1 tsp.)
- Sea salt (to taste)
- Medium carrots (2)
- Bay leaves (2)
- Cayenne pepper (1 tsp.)
- Fresh cilantro (.5 cup)

Preparation Technique:
1. Dice the tomatoes, garlic, onions, and carrots.
2. Rinse and drain the beans. Cook until tender.
3. Warm up the oil and combine each of the fixings into the pan.
4. Add water to reach the desired consistency. Don't boil.
5. Serve while it's hot.

Tuscan Bean Soup

Total Yields Provided: 6 Servings

Ingredient List:
- Medium onion (1)
- Celery (2 stalks)
- Cloves of garlic (4)
- Carrot (1)
- Tomatoes (3 cups)
- Canned cannellini beans (6 cups)
- Water (5 cups)
- Himalayan Salt (.5 tsp.)
- Freshly ground pepper (as desired)
- Quinoa (.5 cup)
- Fresh basil leaves (.25 cup)
- Olive oil (2 tbsp.)

Preparation Technique:
1. Prep the veggies. Chop the celery, carrots, garlic, and tomatoes. Coarsely chop the leaves of basil.
2. In a large skillet, with a couple of teaspoons of water, saute the onions, celery, and garlic until tender.
3. Stir in the chopped tomatoes (juice also) and carrots. Warm it up using the low to medium heat setting.
4. Break up the tomatoes into small chunks. Simmer for 15 to 20 minutes.
5. Stir in the cannellini beans, salt, pepper, and water. Simmer for an additional 20 minutes.

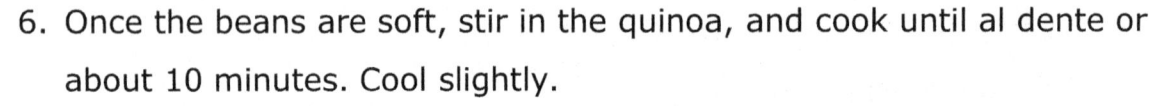

6. Once the beans are soft, stir in the quinoa, and cook until al dente or about 10 minutes. Cool slightly.
7. Serve with a spritz of olive oil along with the basil leaves.

Vegetable Soup

Total Yields Provided: 2 Servings

Ingredient List:
- Brown onion (1)
- Garlic (2 cloves)
- Carrots (2)
- Cauliflower (.25 of 1 head)
- Broccoli (.25 of 1 head)
- Cabbage - any green variety (.25 of 1 head)
- Vegetable stock (1 cup)
- Organic chopped tomatoes (1 can or 8 fresh tomatoes or as desired)
- Himalayan pink salt & Black pepper (to taste)
- Turmeric root (.5-inch root or 1 tsp. dried)
- Ginger root (.5-inch root or 1 tsp. dried)
- Coconut oil

Raw Recipe Ingredients:
- Cucumber (.5 of 1)
- Tomatoes (3)
- Spinach (1 handful)
- Basil (.5 of 1 bunch)
- Coriander (.25 of 1 bunch)
- Chickpeas - garbanzos (.5 to 1 can as desired)

Preparation Technique:
1. Roughly chop the cabbage. Dice the carrots, garlic, and onions. Chop the tomatoes. Prepare the broccoli and cauliflower florets.

2. Sauté the garlic and onions in a portion of coconut oil. After three minutes, toss in the cauliflower, carrots, cabbage, and broccoli. Simmer for another three minutes.
3. Pour in the stock and tomatoes/can of tomatoes. Simmer for 20 to 25 minutes until the veggies are softened.
4. Toss the raw foods into a blender and pulse until smooth.
5. After the soup has simmered for about 20 minutes, transfer it in batches and blend it all together until creamy smooth. It may take a couple of batches into the blender.
6. Serve with a sprig of coriander or basil and enjoy warm.

Salad Options

Apple & Avocado Sesame Salad

Total Yields Provided: 2 Servings

Ingredient List:
- Green apple (1)
- Lemon juice (2 tbsp.)
- Toasted sesame oil (1 tbsp.)
- Onion powder (.25 tsp.)
- Celtic sea salt (.25 tsp. + more to serve)
- Garlic powder (.25 tsp.)
- Red pepper flakes (1 pinch)
- Avocado (1 - skin on)
- Cilantro (1 tsp.)
- Fresh ginger (1.5 tsp.)
- Sesame seeds (.5 tsp.)

Preparation Technique:
1. Squeeze the lemon. Finely dice the apple and ginger. Combine with the lemon juice, sesame oil, onion powder, red pepper flakes, salt, and garlic powder.
2. Slice the avocado into half. Take equal parts of the apple mixture to fill each avocado cavity.
3. Top it off with chopped cilantro and sesame seeds.
4. Enjoy right away for the best taste rewards.

Avocado Salad

Total Yields Provided: 2 Servings

Ingredient List:
- Tortillas (2)
- Firm tofu (.5 of 1 pkg.)
- Avocado (1)
- Pink grapefruit (1)
- Almonds (1 handful)
- Baby spinach (4 handfuls)
- Chili sauce (1 tbsp.)
- Tomatoes (2)
- Red onion (.5 of 1)
- Lemon (.5 of 1)

Preparation Technique:
1. Bake the tortillas for 8 to 10 minutes at 350° Fahrenheit.
2. Chop the onions, tofu, and tomatoes on one side. Mix with a portion of chili sauce.
3. Place it inside the fridge and let it cool.
4. Chop the grapefruit, almonds, and avocado.
5. Mix it together in a serving platter.
6. Spritz with the fresh lemon juice before serving.

Barley & Fresh Papaya Salad With Nuts - Lime & Chili

Total Yields Provided: 4 Servings

Ingredient List:
- Raw barley grains (1 cup)
- Boiling water (2 cups)
- Organic sea salt (1 tsp.)
- Papaya (4 cups)
- Garlic (4 tsp.)
- Raw cashew nuts (4 tbsp.)
- Ginger root (4 tsp.)
- Fresh red chili (4 tsp.)
- Desiccated coconut (4 tbsp.)
- Coriander leaves (4 tbsp.)

Preparation Technique - The Barley:

1. Dice the papaya. Finely chop the garlic and ginger root. Remove the seeds from the chili and finely chop. Roughly chop the cashews and coriander leaves.
2. Toss the barley into a saucepan with boiling water and salt.
3. Once boiling, reduce to a simmer for approximately 50 minutes until the barley is fluffy and has absorbed all the water. Set aside to cool.

Preparation Technique - The Salad:

1. Using four separate serving bowls, add the following fixings:
    a. Cooked - cooled barley (.5 cup)
    b. Chopped coriander leaves (1 tbsp.)
    c. Freshly diced papaya (1 cup)
    d. Freshly chopped ginger (1 tsp.)
    e. Freshly minced garlic (1 tsp.)
    f. Freshly chopped red chili (1 tsp.)
2. Toss the ingredients in each bowl together:
    a. Sprinkle the cashew nuts over each bowl (1 tbsp.)
    b. Sprinkle the desiccated coconut over each bowl (1 tbsp.)
3. Serve.

Brussel Sprouts & Almond Salad

Total Yields Provided: 3-4 Servings

Ingredient List:

- Brussel sprouts (3 cups)
- Quinoa (1 cup)
- Finely chopped garlic (1 clove)
- Kale (1 cup)
- Flaked almonds (.33 cup)
- Pomegranate (.5 of 1)
- Chopped fresh parsley (.33 cup)
- Pomegranate molasses (1 tsp.)
- Rice vinegar (1 tsp.)
- Zest of orange (1)
- Ginger (1.5 tsp.)
- Olive oil (1 tbsp.)
- Himalayan salt (1 pinch)

Preparation Technique:

1. Warm up the oven to reach 350° Fahrenheit.
2. Chop the base away from the Brussel sprouts and slice into halves. Toss into the baking pan. Chop the garlic and add to the pan with a sprinkle of salt.
3. Bake for 25 minutes.
4. Prepare the quinoa using the package directions and drain.
5. Chop the kale into three-inch chunks. Cook in boiling salted water for 30 to 40 seconds. Drain well in a colander.

6. In a mixing container, add the blanched kale, roasted Brussel sprouts, and quinoa.
7. Work in the rice vinegar, olive oil, orange zest, grated fresh ginger, pomegranate molasses, and fresh parsley.
8. Brown the flaked almonds in a pan for 1 minute using the low heat setting.
9. Take the pan from the heat. Sprinkle as desired with the pomegranate seeds.
10. Serve the salad hot or cold with a garnish of the pomegranate seeds and flaked almonds.

Chopped Veggie Salad & Quinoa

Total Yields Provided: 4-6 Servings

Ingredient List:
- Quinoa (1 cup)
- Red or yellow bell peppers (2 cups)
- Red onion (.5 cup)
- Cucumber (2 cups)
- Cherry tomatoes (3 cups)
- Freshly squeezed lemon juice (2 tbsp.)
- Black pepper (as desired)
- Sea salt (2 tsp.)
- Water (2 cups)

Preparation Technique:
1. Rinse the quinoa before you get started and let it drain in a strainer.
2. Pour the water in the pan and wait for it to boil. Pour in the quinoa and lower the temperature setting to medium.
3. Prepare the quinoa for 10 to 15 minutes or until the liquid is absorbed. Stir occasionally.
4. Take the pot off the heat and let the quinoa cool. Do *not* rinse the cooked quinoa.
5. Chop the onion, cucumber, and peppers. Cut the cherry tomatoes into halves. Toss the quinoa and the chopped veggies into a salad container and toss well. Add the salt, pepper, and lemon juice.
6. Serve chilled with lemon wedges.

Corn - Heirloom Cherry & Bean Salad

Total Yields Provided: 2 Servings

Ingredient List:
- Freshly picked corn (6 cobs)
- Cherry heirloom tomatoes (32 sliced in half)
- Red onion (.5 cup)
- Fresh cilantro (.66 cup)
- Black pinto beans (2 cans)
- Olive oil (.5 cup)
- Celtic sea salt (1 pinch)
- Lime juice (1)

Preparation Technique:
1. Slice the tomatoes into halves and set aside.
2. Rinse and drain the beans. Prepare a large pot of water. Once boiling, add the cobs to the water to simmer for about 3 to 5 minutes.
3. Remove & place in the cold water to help stop cooking. Slice the kernels of corn off the cob and put into a salad dish. Toss with the diced onion, chopped cilantro, cherry tomatoes, and black beans.
4. Combine the oil, lime juice, with a pinch of salt.
5. Pour over the corn mixture to coat evenly. Let it stand 10 minutes and enjoy.

Creamy Kale Salad With Tomato & Avocado

Total Yields Provided: 1-2 Servings

Ingredient List:
- Kale (2 large handfuls)
- Medium avocado (1 ripe)
- Tomatoes (2 ripe)
- Lime juice (1 lime)
- Crushed garlic (1 clove) OR Garlic powder (.5 tsp.)
- Agave syrup (1 tbsp.)
- Paprika (.5 tsp.)
- Ground black pepper (.5 tsp.)

Preparation Technique:
1. Rinse and roughly chop the kale and tomatoes into a large glass mixing bowl.
2. Peel the avocado and add to the bowl.
3. Juice the lime and add the rest of the fixings. Massage all the ingredients together. Serve.

Cucumber & Tempeh Salad

Total Yields Provided: 3-4 Servings

Ingredient List:
- Cashew nuts (.5 cup)
- Cucumber (1 cup)
- Sprouts (1 large helping)
- Arugula (2 large helpings)
- Red onion (.25 of 1)
- Spring onions (2)
- Coriander (2 tbsp.)
- Tempeh (150g)
- Sunflower oil (1 tsp.)

Ingredient List - The Dressing:
- Himalayan salt (1 pinch)
- Toasted sesame oil (1 tsp.)
- Red chili (.25 of 1 large)
- Garlic (1 clove)
- Rice vinegar (.125 cup)
- Agave syrup (1 tsp.)
- Tamari (1 tsp.)
- Lime juice (1 lime) & finely grated (zest of ½)

Preparation Technique:
1. Finely slice the onions, garlic, red chili, and coriander. Set each veggie aside for now.

2. Prepare the dressing. Mix each of the fixings into a saucepan, except for the lime juice and zest.
3. Simmer for three to four minutes. Set to the side for now.
4. Dry-roast the cashews. Toss them with the sprouts, cucumber, arugula, red onion, coriander, and spring onions.
5. Place the skillet with oil on the heated burner. Continue sautéing the tempeh cubes well done.
6. Toss the tempeh into the salad container and spritz with the juice. Toss the zest to the dressing in the saucepan.
7. Dress the salad and mix well. Scoop it out, serve and enjoy.

Detox Super Salad

Total Yields Provided: 2 loaded salads

Ingredient List:
- Lettuce (1 head)
- Baby kale (1 handful)
- Handful spinach (1 handful)
- Parsley (20 stems)
- Cilantro (20 stems)
- Pea shoots (2 handfuls)
- Sprouts - radish - broccoli or alfalfa - etc. (2 handfuls)
- Carrot (1)
- Cherry tomatoes (12)
- Red cabbage (1 cup)
- Radishes (12)
- Celery (1 stalk)
- Avocado (1)
- Watermelon radish (1 slivered)

Ingredient List - The Dressing:
- Lemon juice (2 lemons)
- Organic virgin olive oil (8 tbsp.)
- Finely minced garlic - not pressed (2 large cloves)
- Fresh ground black pepper (as desired)
- Himalayan salt (2 pinches)
- Liquid alcohol-free stevia (2 drops) or Maple syrup or both (1 tsp.)

Preparation Technique:
1. Prepare and whisk the dressing so the flavors can mingle.
2. Toss the greens into a serving bowl as the base of your salad.
3. Arrange all of the veggies in the little groupings around the perimeter.
4. Add the radish at the center.
5. Serve with the dressing.
6. Toss the salad well.

Healthy Side Salad

Total Yields Provided: 2 Servings

Ingredient List:
- Little gem butterhead lettuces (2)
- Radishes (2)
- Cucumber (.5 of 1)
- Carrot (.5 of 1)
- Tomatoes (2)
- Avocado (1)
- Olive oil
- Lemon (.5 of 1 - juiced)

Preparation Technique:
1. Chop the radishes and dice the tomatoes and avocado. Slice the cucumber and cut the carrots into matchsticks. Separate the leaves and fill with the chopped salad ingredients.
2. Drizzle with a spritz of olive oil, a squeeze of fresh lemon, and serve.
3. *Tip*: If you want to increase the omega 3 content, swap the olive oil for flax oil or make a mix of 50/50 of each.

Jicama & Fennel Salad

Total Yields Provided: 2 large servings

Ingredient List:
- Radishes (3)
- Fennel bulb (1 large)
- Medium jicama (.5 of 1)
- Celery (3 stalks)
- Lime juice (1 lime)
- Avocado oil (.25 cup)
- Salt (A pinch)
- Macadamia nuts - for the topping

Preparation Technique:
1. Cut away the greens from the fennel. Peel and cut the jicama into half.
2. Using a mandolin slicer (thinnest setting); slice the radish, jicama, celery, and fennel.
3. Toss into a bowl with the oil and juice.
4. Sprinkle with a pinch of salt and a topping of chopped macadamia nuts before serving.

Julienne Salad Of Parsnip - Apple & Celeriac

Total Yields Provided: 1 large/2 small servings

Ingredient List:
- Lemon juice (.75 if 1 lemon + .25 tsp. zest)
- Cashew nut (.125 cup)
- Cold-pressed olive oil (.125 cup)
- Zucchini (.125 cup)
- Fresh thyme leaves (.5 tsp.)
- Pink peppercorns (10 + a few for garnish)
- Stevia (1-2 drops) or Maple syrup (.5 tsp.)
- Apple (.5 of 1) resting in lemon water (the juice of 1/2 more lemon in 1-2 cups of water)
- Celery (.5 of 1 medium)
- Parsnip (1)
- Pea shoots
- Baby greens
- Himalayan salt (large pinch)
- Raw pine nuts (.125 cup)

Preparation Technique:
1. Peel and dice the zucchini. Julienne cut the apple, parsnip, and celery.
2. Prepare the dressing. Combine olive oil, zucchini, lemon juice, cashews, thyme, stevia, peppercorns, and maple syrup. Mix until creamy and smooth.
3. Toss the julienne slices with dressing. Pile upon pea shoots & the baby greens

4. Garnish with some pink peppercorns, pine nuts, and a sprig of thyme.

Kale Caesar Salad

Total Yields Provided: 2 Servings

Ingredient List:
- Curly kale (1 large)
- Sunflower seeds (1 cup + garnish if desired)
- Raw almond nuts (.33 cup)
- Chipotle powder or to your liking (.125 tsp.)
- Smoked paprika (.5 tsp.)
- Garlic (2 cloves)
- Filtered water (1.25 cups)
- Agave syrup (1.5 tsp.) or rice malt syrup
- Sea salt (.5 tsp.)

Preparation Technique:
1. Rinse and pat dry kale leaves. Discard the membrane centers. Tear the kale into small pieces and add to a large container.
2. Add the remainder of the fixings into the blender.
3. Mix until creamy and smooth.
4. Pour half the mixture over the prepared leaves. Toss well to coat.
5. Add the remainder of the mixture to thoroughly cover the leaves really well.
6. Set it aside for about ten minutes.
7. Serve with a sprinkle of sunflower seeds to your liking.

Lentil & Beet Salad

Total Yields Provided: 2 Servings

Ingredient List:
- Red beets (2 large)
- Black dried beluga lentils (1.5 cups)
- Capers (.5 cup)
- Chopped basil (.25 cup)
- Soy yogurt (1 cup)
- Fresh sprouts or microgreens (1 cup)

Ingredient List - The Dressing:
- Clove of garlic (1 large)
- Meyer lemon (1 large)
- Olive oil (.25 cup)
- Coriander powder (1 tsp.)
- Sea salt (1 tsp.)
- Clove powder (1 pinch)
- Freshly cracked black pepper (as desired)

Preparation Technique:
1. Soak the lentils overnight in a pan or other container to decrease the cooking time. Rinse and drain well before cooking.
2. Zest and juice the lemon.
3. Empty the water into a large pot to boil. Toss the beets into the pot.
4. Cover with a lid. Cook until they're tender on low for 35 to 40 minutes.

5. Remove from the water and remove the skins to cut into cubes and set aside.
6. While the beets are cooking, bring the water to a boil in another medium pot. Prepare the lentils with a dusting of salt. Cook for 10 to 15 minutes, making sure they're firm, not overcooked. Transfer from the heat and drain before the skins are falling off.
7. Combine all of the dressing fixings in a small mason jar.
8. Put a top on the jar and shake until well combined. Adjust the seasonings to taste. Store in the fridge.
9. *To Assemble*: Combine the cubed beets, capers, cooked lentils, and basil in a bowl. Toss with vinaigrette.
10. Serve with a big handful of microgreens and a dollop of yogurt.
11. If desired, flavor it up with a sprinkle of pepper and salt.

Lentil Salad

Total Yields Provided: 2-4 Servings

Ingredient List:
- Celery (2 cups)
- Sesame tahini - raw (1 tbsp.)
- Lentil sprouts (5 cups)
- Bragg's Aminos (3 tbsp.)
- Red pepper (1)
- Green onions with tops (2)
- Fresh chives (2 tbsp.)
- Raw almond butter (1 cup)
- Olive oil (4 tbsp.)
- *Optional*: Kelp (2 tsp.)

Preparation Technique:
1. Mince the celery, chives, and onions. Chop the red pepper. Soak the lentils overnight and thoroughly rinse before preparing.
2. For the dressing, blend the almond butter, olive oil, and alkaline water until smooth.
3. Split the lentil sprouts in a food processor or chop finely by hand. Toss into a large salad bowl.
4. Add the rest of the fixings, adding the almond butter mixture on the top.
5. *Note:* Stir the mixture well. Chill for several hours before serving.

Roasted Sweet Potato Salad

Total Yields Provided: 6 Servings

Ingredient List:
- Olive oil (3 tbsp.)
- Sweet potatoes (3)
- Salt (1 tsp.)
- Ground ginger (1 tsp.)
- Mango chutney (2 tbsp.)
- Dijon mustard (1 tbsp.)
- Cumin (1 tsp.)
- Garlic clove (1 tsp.)
- Balsamic vinegar (3 tbsp.)
- Olive oil (2 tbsp.)
- Scallions (1 cup)
- Toasted sliced almonds (.5 cup)
- Dried cranberries (.5 cup)

Preparation Technique:
1. Warm up the oven to reach 425° Fahrenheit.
2. Cover a large baking tin with a sheet of aluminum foil.
3. Use a sharp knife to peel and dice the potatoes into one-inch cubes. Mince the garlic and chop the scallions.
4. Scoop up the potatoes and mix with the olive oil, cumin, ginger, and salt onto the baking sheet.
5. Roast until the potatoes are tender (approx. 30 min.). Stir occasionally for even roasting.

6. Whisk the garlic, with the mustard, chutney, vinegar, and olive oil in a bowl.
7. Transfer the potatoes to the stovetop to cool slightly (approximately ten min.).
8. Toss the potatoes with the dressing mixture.
9. Serve with a garnish of the almond either hot or at room temperature.

Savory Sweet Salad

Total Yields Provided: 2-4 Servings

Ingredient List:
- Butter lettuce (1 large head)
- Cucumber (.5 of 1)
- Pomegranate - seeded (1) or .33 cup seeds
- Avocado (1)
- Pistachios (.25 cup)

Ingredient List - Dressing:
- Apple cider vinegar (.25 cup)
- Olive oil - extra-virgin (.5 cup)
- Garlic clove (1)

Preparation Technique:
1. Tear the lettuce pieces.
2. Shell and chop the pistachios, cube the avocado, and slice the cucumber. Mince the garlic.
3. Prepare the dressing.
4. Lunch or dinner is served.

Spanish Bean Salad

Total Yields Provided: 3-4 Servings

Ingredient List:

- Pinto beans (8 oz.)
- Chickpeas (8 oz.)
- Cannellini beans (8 oz.)
- Red bell pepper (.5 of 1)
- Carrot (1)
- Celery (1 stalk
- Olive oil (.25 cup)
- Optional: Flax oil (1 tbsp.)
- Optional: Hemp oil (.5 tbsp.)
- Lemon juice (1 tbsp.)
- Lime juice (1 tbsp.)
- Agave syrup (1 tbsp.)
- Celtic sea salt (.25 tbsp.)
- Garlic (1 clove)
- Fresh cilantro (.125 cup)
- Ground cumin (.25 tbsp.)
- Black pepper (.5 tsp.)
- Chili powder (.5 tsp.)
- Cayenne pepper (as desired)
- *Optional*: Green onion chopped (as desired)

Preparation Technique:

1. Rinse and drain the canned beans. Chop the carrot, celery, onions, cilantro, and bell pepper. Mince the garlic.

2. Combine the beans, green onions, and chopped veggies.
3. Whisk the rest of the fixings (a large mixing cup is excellent).
4. Pour the dressing over the vegetables and gently combine them without mashing the beans.
5. Serve over fresh greens. Season with cayenne pepper.

Spring Beluga Lentil & Beet Salad With Coriander Vinaigrette

Total Yields Provided: 2 Servings

Ingredient List - The Salad:

- Red beets (2 large)
- Black dried beluga lentils (1.5 cups)
- Capers (.5 cup)
- Chopped basil (.25 cup)
- Soy yogurt (1 cup)
- Fresh sprouts or microgreens (1 cup)

Ingredient List - The Dressing:

- Clove of garlic (1 large)
- Meyer lemon (1 large)
- Olive oil (.25 cup)
- Coriander powder (1 tsp.)
- Sea salt (1 tsp.)
- Clove powder (1 pinch)
- Freshly cracked black pepper (as desired)

Preparation Technique:

1. Soak the lentils overnight in a pan or other container to decrease the cooking time. Rinse and drain well before cooking.
2. Zest and juice the lemon.
3. Empty the water into a large pot to boil. Toss the beets into the pot.
4. Cover with a lid. Cook until they're tender on low for 35 to 40 minutes.
5. Remove from the water, and remove the skins to cut into cubes and set aside.

6. While the beets are cooking, bring water to a boil in another medium pot. Prepare the lentils with a pinch of salt. Cook for 10 to 15 minutes, making sure they're firm - not overcooked. Transfer from the heat and drain before the skins are falling off.
7. Prepare the dressing. Combine all of the fixings in a small mason jar. Place a top on the jar and shake until well combined. Adjust seasonings to taste. Store in the fridge until ready to use.
8. *To Assemble*: Combine the cubed beets, capers, cooked lentils, and basil in a bowl. Toss with vinaigrette.
9. Serve with a big handful of microgreens and a dollop of yogurt.
10. If desired, flavor it up with a sprinkle of pepper and salt.

Summer Salad With Mint & Lemon Dressing

Servings Provided: 4 Servings

Ingredients Needed:
- Avocado (1)
- Bunches of asparagus (2-3)
- Cilantro/Coriander (.5 of 1 bunch)
- Flat-leaf parsley (.5 of 1 bunch)
- Radish (5)
- Cooked green peas (1 cup)
- Zucchini (2)

Ingredients Needed - The Dressing:
- Lemons (3 juiced)
- Shallots (2)
- Garlic (1 clove)
- Olive or flax oil or a combination (1 cup)
- Dijon mustard (1 tbsp.)
- Mint (.25 of 1 bunch)
- Himalayan salt & Black pepper (to your liking)

Preparation Technique:
1. Roughly chop the mint, cilantro, and parsley. Thinly slice the radishes and zucchini with a vegetable peeler. Slice the avocado. Dice the shallots and crush the garlic.
2. Blanch the asparagus. Place it into boiling water for 1 minute.

3. Drain and rinse under cold water. Slice along the length to create long strips.
4. Gently sauté the zucchini in a griddle pan until it's just starting to brown.
5. Assemble the salad by combining the avocado, zucchini, asparagus, cilantro, parsley, radish, and peas in a large salad bowl.
6. Prepare the dressing by blending each of the fixings in a blender or food processor.
7. Dress and season to taste.
8. The dressing will keep for up to a week in an airtight container in the refrigerator.

Tomato & Avocado Salad

Total Yields Provided: 1 Serving

Ingredient List:
- Tomato (.5 of 1)
- Ripe avocado (.5 of 1 large)
- Medium English cucumber (.5 of 1)
- Red bell pepper (.5 of 1)
- Lemon or lime - juiced (.5 of 1)
- Raw tahini sauce (.125 cup)
- Olive oil (1 to 2 tbsp.)
- Real salt (.125 tsp.)

Preparation Technique:
1. Finely chop the veggies.
2. Combine all of the fixings and serve.

Zesty Alkaline Salad Brussels & Kale

Total Yields Provided: 4 Servings

Ingredient List:
- Tuscan kale (2 large bunches)
- Brussels sprouts (15)
- Raw almonds (.33 cup)
- Pine nuts (2 tbsp.)
- Pomegranate seeds (2 tbsp.)
- Himalayan pink salt (to your liking)
- Coarse ground black pepper (.125 tsp. or to taste)
- Minced shallots (1 tbsp.)
- Garlic (2 small cloves)
- Dijon mustard (2 tbsp.)
- Olive oil (.25 cup)
- Agave Syrup (1 tsp.)
- Freshly squeezed lemon juice (.25 cup)
- Mint leaves (8)

Preparation Technique:
1. Mince the garlic cloves and chop the mint leaves.
2. Prepare the salad dressing and gently whisk together.
3. Rinse the kale and remove the thick stem. Roll and finely slice the leaves into ribbons.
4. Finely slice the brussels sprouts.
5. Put both greens into a serving bowl.

6. Roughly chop the almonds and toss into the salad along with the pomegranate seeds and pine nuts.
7. Add the dressing in small portions and toss.
8. It will keep for at least 24 hours (even fully dressed).

Chapter 4: Delicious Beverages & Smoothies

Milk Options

<u>*Strawberry Rose Almond Milk*</u>

Total Yields Provided: 6 cups

Ingredient List:

- Raw almonds (1 cup)
- Filtered water (3 cups)
- Sea salt (1 tsp.)
- Chopped pitted dates (.25 cup)
- Fresh strawberries (3 cups)
- Pure rosewater (2 tsp.)

Preparation Technique:

1. Soak the almonds. Pour the nuts into a glass dish and add the water. Add the salt and splash of juice/vinegar and salt. Place a lid on the dish and soak for about 12 hours.
2. Drain and rinse the almonds several times.
3. Pour the rinsed almonds and clean water into the blender.
4. Pulse using the high setting for no more than one minute or until the nuts are completely granulated.
5. Strain using a nut milk bag (knee-high nylon hosiery will also work) over the opening of a glass jar.
6. Pour the milk into the bag. Twist the bag closed. Gently squeeze it to pass the liquid through (via the almond pulp).
7. Rinse the blender container and pour the strained milk back in.
8. Toss in the strawberries, rosewater, dates, and salt. Blend using the high speed for 30 to 60 seconds until creamy.
9. It will keep for two to three days in a cold fridge.

Turmeric Milk

Total Yields Provided: 2 Servings

Ingredient List:
- Filtered water (3 cups)
- Raw almonds (1 cup)
- Firmly packed chopped - pitted dates (.25 cup)
- Ground turmeric (1 tbsp.)
- Natural vanilla extract (1 tsp.)
- Cinnamon (1 tsp.)
- Fresh minced ginger (1 tsp.)
- Ground cardamom (.25 tsp.)
- Black pepper (.125 tsp.)
- Sea salt (1 pinch)

Preparation Technique:

1. Soak the almonds for 8 hours.
2. Drain and rinse the soaked almonds. Discard the soaking liquid.
3. Transfer the drained almonds into the blender.
4. Pour in the water. Pulse on high for approximately 30-60 seconds or until the almonds are of a fine texture.
5. Strain the almond milk with a nut milk bag or filtration bag. You can also use a piece of hosiery in an emergency.
6. Wash your blender container. Pour in the strained milk.
7. Add the dates (or birch xylitol and stevia), ginger, turmeric, vanilla, cardamom, cinnamon, black pepper, and salt.
8. Pulse using the high setting for 10 to 20 seconds until the mixture is smooth and creamy.
9. Transfer to a sealed glass jar. Chill in the fridge, and serve chilled.
10. If you prefer it warm, gently warm on the stovetop using low heat.
11. The milk will keep in the refrigerator for two to three days.

Walnut Milk

Total Yields Provided: 3.5 cups

Ingredient List -Unsweetened Milk:

- Soaked raw walnuts (1 cup)
- Filtered water (3 cups)
- Sea salt (A pinch)

Ingredient List - Sweetened Milk:

- Pitted dates (3-4) or Pure maple syrup (2-3 tbsp.)
- Pure vanilla extract (1 tsp.)
- *Optional*: Sunflower lecithin (1 tbsp.)

Preparation Technique:

1. Soak the almonds as shown in *Strawberry Rose Almond Milk* (step 1-6).
2. Combine the above fixings in the blender and pulse until creamy.
3. It will be fresh for up to three days in the refrigerator.
4. Note: If the milk wasn't soaked, it would last for about five days.

Tea Options

Alkaline Detox Tea

Total Yields Provided: 1-2 Servings

Ingredient List:
- Cardamom powder (.25 tsp.)
- Ginger powder (.5 tsp.
- Cinnamon (.25 tsp.)
- Turmeric powder (.5 tsp.)
- Filtered water (2 cups)
- Lemon (.5 of 1)

Preparation Technique:
1. Warm the water in a saucepan.
2. Add the spices (turmeric, ginger, and cardamom). Squeeze and add the lemon as desired.
3. Stir and enjoy your tea.

Turmeric 'Bulletproof' Tea

Total Yields Provided: 2 Servings

Ingredient List:
- Fresh turmeric (1-inch)
- Fresh ginger sliced (1-inch)
- Coconut oil (1 tbsp.)
- Coconut or almond milk (16 oz.)
- Powdered cinnamon (1 tsp.)
- Maca powder (1 tsp. - optional)
- Coconut syrup or rice malt syrup optional (1 tsp.)

Preparation Technique:
1. Slice the turmeric and ginger and put into a saucepan with the milk, coconut oil, cinnamon, maca, and syrup if using.
2. Simmer for 5 to 10 minutes for the ginger and turmeric to infuse.
3. Pour everything into a high-powered blender such as a Nutribullet or Vitamix. Blend on the high-speed setting for 30 seconds to liquefy the turmeric and ginger and create a nice froth on the tea. Serve.

Other Delicious Options

Banana Milkshake

Total Yields Provided: 2 Servings

Ingredient List:
- Baby bananas (6 frozen)
- Coconut - Hemp or Walnut milk (.25 cup)
- Agave (1 tbsp.)
- Cloves (.125 tsp.)

Preparation Technique:
1. Toss all of the fixings into a blender. Combine until creamy smooth.
2. Add more milk if needed to improve the consistency.
3. Enjoy your shake.

Calm Down Adrenal-Healing Juice

Total Yields Provided: 2 Servings

Ingredient List:
- Basil leaves (1 handful)
- Carrots (2)
- Watercress or other leafy green (1 handful)
- Cucumber (1 large)
- Spinach (1 handful)
- Chia seeds (2 tbsp.)
- Bell pepper (.5 of 1)
- *Optional:* Coconut water (.75 to 1 cup)

Preparation Technique:
1. Wash and juice all of the ingredients except the chia seeds.
2. After juicing all of the veggies, stir in the chia seeds. Soak for 8 to 10 minutes for the chia to swell.
3. Stir again and serve.

Fat Flush Juice

Total Yields Provided: 2 Servings

Ingredient List:
- Baby spinach (3 large handfuls)
- Kale - can be any variety (.5 of 1 bunch)
- Beetroot & leaves if possible (1 medium)
- Cucumber (1)
- Powdered cinnamon (.5 tsp.)

Preparation Technique:
1. Wash, chop, and juice all of the fixings. Omit the cinnamon.
2. Run around .5 cup of water through the juicer to slightly dilute the juice and help with the juicer cleaning process.
3. Whisk the cinnamon into the juice and serve.

Green Fruit Juice

Total Yields Provided: 2 Servings

Ingredient List:
- Peeled & chopped kiwis (4 large)
- Cored & sliced green apples (2 large)
- Seedless green grapes (1 cup)
- Lime juice (2 tsp.)

Preparation Technique:
1. Toss each of the fixings into a juicer. Extract the juice.
2. Transfer to two glasses and enjoy immediately for the best taste results.

Green Power Shake

Total Yields Provided: 1-2 Servings

Ingredient List:
- Avocado (1)
- Cucumber (.5 of 1 medium)
- Cabbage (1 cup)
- Fresh spinach leaves (1 cup)
- Peeled lime (1)
- SuperGreens Powder/your favorite (1 tbsp.)
- Ice cubes - Alkaline water is best (as desired)

Preparation Technique:
1. Toss each of the fixings into the blender except for the SuperGreens powder.
2. Pulse until smooth.
3. Serve with ice cubes as desired.

High-Potassium Juice

Total Yields Provided: 2 Servings

Ingredient List:
- Cucumber (1)
- Celery (2 sticks)
- Spinach (.33 cup)
- Kale (.33 cup)
- Bell pepper (.5 of 1)
- Carrots (2)
- Coconut water or filtered water (as needed)

Preparation Technique:
1. Rinse, chop, and juice the fixings.
2. Serve with a squeeze of fresh lemon if it's too green-tasting.

Hypothyroidism Re-Balance Juice

Total Yields Provided: 2 Servings

Ingredient List:
- Celery (2 stalks)
- Torn lettuce leaves (2 big handfuls)
- Coriander/cilantro (.5 of 1 bunch)
- Arugula/rocket leaves (.5 cup)
- Cucumber (1)

Preparation Technique:
1. Toss each of the fixings into your blender.
2. Pulse and serve.

Kiwi & Strawberry Popsicles

Total Yields Provided: 8 Servings

Ingredient List:
- Medium to large strawberries (8)
- Kiwi fruit (.5 of 1)
- Popsicle mold (silicone molds work the best)

Preparation Technique:
1. Remove the tops of the strawberries and cut out the hulls. Cut the strawberries into small pieces. Put them in a small food processor with a teaspoon of agave nectar.
2. Pulse just until almost smooth, leaving a few small chunks if desired.
3. Cut the kiwi fruit in half. Scoop out the fruit from each half carefully using a spoon. Slice into half circles.
4. Lay a few slices of kiwi fruit in the popsicle mold and add a few tablespoons of strawberry puree until the mold is half full. Add the rest until the mold is full.
5. Cover the mold and freeze for at least two hours.
6. *Note:* You can omit the agave nectar if the berries are sweet and very ripe.

Non-Dairy Apple Parfait

Total Yields Provided: 1 Serving

Ingredient List:

- Soaked raw cashews (.5 cup)
- Unsweetened coconut or almond milk (.5 cup)
- Vanilla (.5 tsp.)
- Rolled gluten-free oats, uncooked (.33 cup)
- Chopped apple (1 cup)
- Hemp seeds (1 tbsp.)
- *Also Needed*: Blender

Preparation Technique:

1. Soak the cashews for 20 minutes to one hour.
2. Blend the almond milk, cashews, and vanilla.
3. Mix until creamy textured.
4. Chop the apple.
5. Layer the fixings in a dessert cup: Add a plentiful spoonful of the cashew cream, and another spoonful of apples.
6. Top it off with the hemp seeds and oats before serving.

Soy Cucumber Shake

Total Yields Provided: 1-2 Servings

Ingredient List:
- Unsweetened soy milk (2 cups)
- Unsweetened coconut milk (.25 cup)
- Small cucumbers (2 shredded)
- Organic vanilla (1 tsp.)
- Ice cubes - best made with alkaline water (6-8)

Preparation Technique:
1. Finely shred the cucumbers.
2. Toss all of the fixings into a blender.
3. Mix for just under a minute.

Smoothie Options

Almond & Avocado Green Smoothie

Total Yields Provided: 2 Servings

Ingredient List:
- Avocado (.5 of 1)
- Kale (1 handful)
- Sesame seeds (1 tbsp.)
- Almonds (1 tbsp.)
- Cucumber (1)
- Spinach (1 handful)
- Pumpkin seeds (1 tbsp.)
- Handful swiss chard/Beet greens or other greens
- Filtered water - Almond or coconut milk (1 cup)

Preparation Technique:
1. Blend together all ingredients until smooth.
2. Pour in the coconut water or filtered water at the end to get to the desired consistency.

Banana Smoothie

Total Yields Provided: 2 Servings

Ingredient List:
- Unsweetened chilled almond milk (2 cups)
- Large frozen banana (1 large)
- Almonds (1 tbsp.)
- Organic vanilla extract (1 tsp.)

Preparation Technique:
1. Peel and slice the frozen banana. Chop the almonds.
2. Toss all of the fixings into a high-speed blender. Pulse.
3. When creamy smooth, pour into two chilled glasses.
4. Enjoy immediately.

Banana - Berry Green Smoothie

Total Yields Provided: 2 Servings

Ingredient List:
- Unsweetened almond milk (2 cups)
- Fresh spinach (2 cups)
- Frozen banana (1)
- Frozen mixed berries (1 cup)
- Coconut oil (1 tbsp.)
- Cinnamon (.5 tsp.)
- Raw almond butter (2 tbsp.)

Preparation Technique:
1. Rinse the fruit and veggies.
2. Add the almond milk and spinach into the blender.
3. Blend in the remainder of the fixings and mix well before serving.

Banana - Cacao Smoothie

Total Yields Provided: 1 Serving

Ingredient List:
- Banana (1)
- Your choice plant milk (2 cups)
- Agave nectar (1 tsp.)
- Raw cacao powder (2 tsp.)
- Cinnamon (1 pinch)
- Crushed ice (to your liking)

Preparation Technique:
1. Combine each of the fixings.
2. Serve and enjoy anytime!

Chili Chai Hot Chocolate

Total Yields Provided: 2 Servings

Ingredient List:
- Coconut or almond milk (2 cups)
- Almond butter (1 tbsp.)
- Organic cacao powder (2 tbsp.)
- Cinnamon powder (1 tsp.)
- Root ginger (1-inch-sliced)
- Cardamom powder (1 tsp.)
- Red chili (1 or more - as desired)
- Coconut or MCT oil (1 tbsp.)

Preparation Technique:
1. Slice the ginger and add the milk, almond butter, cacao, spices, and oil to a saucepan.
2. Simmer for 5 to 10 minutes.
3. Transfer to a blender. Use the high-speed setting to mix until smooth and a froth has formed.
4. Sprinkle with cinnamon, serve and enjoy!

Crunch Berry Smoothie

Total Yields Provided: 1-2 servings

Ingredient List:
- Frozen & peeled banana (1)
- Fresh spinach (2 cups)
- Almond milk - unsweet (2 cups)
- Your choice of frozen mixed berries - grapes or strawberries (1 cup)
- Raw almond butter (4 tbsp.)
- Chia (1 tbsp.)

Preparation Technique:
1. Blend the spinach and almond milk first.
2. Then, add the rest of the fixings except chia.
3. Blend using the low-speed setting.
4. Add the chia once all fixings are smooth.
5. The seeds need to expand. Let the mixture rest for a few minutes before serving.

Grape - Parsley & Lemonade Smoothie

Total Yields Provided: 2 Servings

Ingredient List:
- Fresh lemon juice (.25 cup)
- Green seedless grapes (3 cups)
- Flat-leaf parsley (1 medium bunch)
- Avocado (.5 of 1 small)
- Liquid stevia (5 drops + more if desired)
- Ice cubes (2 cups)

Ingredient List - Optional Boosters:
- Minced ginger (2 tsp.)
- Flax oil (1 tsp.)
- Wheatgrass powder (1 tsp.)

Preparation Technique:
1. Remove the pit from the avocado and peel. Chop the parsley and mince the ginger (if using).
2. Toss in each of the fixings into the blender (including any boosters).
3. Work it using the high setting for 30 to 60 seconds until frosty.

Grapefruit & Green Tea Smoothie

Total Yields Provided: Two 16 oz. Servings

Ingredient List:

- Unsweetened brewed green tea - chilled (.75 cup)
- Ruby red grapefruit (1 cup)
- Green apple (1)
- Baby spinach (1 cup)
- Medium avocado (.5 of 1)
- Frozen pineapple (2 cups)
- Red pepper flakes or cayenne pepper (1 pinch)

Ingredient List - Optional Boosters:

- Flax oil (1 tbsp.)
- Matcha powder (1 tsp.)
- Chia seeds (1 tbsp.)

Preparation Technique:

1. Peel and section the grapefruit. Core and quarter the apple.
2. Remove the pit from the avocado and peel.
3. Scoop the fixings together and toss into the blender.
4. Pulse using the high function for 30 seconds to one minute or until smooth.

Lime Avocado Smoothie

Total Yields Provided: 1 Serving

Ingredient List:
- Cucumber with peel (.75 cup)
- Baby spinach (3 cups)
- Frozen broccoli (2 cups)
- Avocado (.5 of 1 medium)
- Organic silken tofu (.5 cup)
- Lime (2 small or 1 large)
- Stevia extract (.25 tsp.)
- Ice (.5 cup)
- Unsweetened organic plant-based milk (.5 cup)

Preparation Technique:
1. Peel the limes and toss with the rest of the fixings into a powerful high-speed blender.
2. Blend until smooth and creamy.
3. Serve when ready.

Mango Express Smoothies

Total Yields Provided: 2 Servings

Ingredient List:
- Frozen mango (2 cups)
- Almond butter (.25 cup)
- Ground turmeric (1 pinch)
- Freshly squeezed lemon juice (2 tbsp.)
- Unsweetened almond milk (1.25 cups)
- Ice cubes (25 cups)

Preparation Technique:
1. Peel and remove the pit from the mango. Chop it to bits.
2. Toss everything into a high-power blender. Pulse until creamy.
3. Pour into a couple of chilled mugs and enjoy right away.

Mint Chocolate Ice Cream Smoothie

Total Yields Provided: 1-2 Servings

Ingredient List:
- Frozen ripe bananas (4)
- Medjool dates (2 large or 4 small)
- Carob powder (1 tsp.)
- Almond milk (approx. 7 oz.)
- Fresh mint leaves (2-3 sprigs)
- Ice cubes

Preparation Technique:
1. Toss each of the fixings into a high-speed blender and blend for one to two minutes.
2. Adjust the liquids as needed with ice or water.
3. Top it off with a sprig of mint.

Pineapple Green Smoothie

Total Yields Provided: 1 Serving

Ingredient List:
- Lime (1)
- Apples (2)
- Cucumber (1-inch slices)
- Celery stick (.5 of 1)
- Kale or Spinach (1 handful)
- Pineapple (1-inch slices)
- Wheatgrass powder (1 tsp.)
- Water (as needed)
- *Optional:* Spirulina powder (.5 tsp.)
- *Optional*: Avocado (.5 of 1)

Preparation Technique:
1. Wash ingredients. Chop the apples. Slice the cucumber into 1-inch slices.
2. Toss everything into the blender. Thin with water as needed.
3. Blend, pour, drink, and enjoy.

Raspberry & Tofu Smoothie

Total Yields Provided: 2 Servings

Ingredient List:
- Drained firm silken tofu (6 oz.)
- Fresh raspberries (1.5 cups)
- Coconut extract (.125 tsp.)
- Powdered stevia (1 tsp.)
- Almond milk - unsweetened (1.5 cups)
- Crushed ice cubes (.25 cup)

Preparation Technique:
1. Drain the tofu.
2. Combine all of the fixings in a high-speed blender. Pulse until creamy.
3. Pour the delicious smoothie into two glasses and serve.

Spicy Gazpacho Grab Smoothies

Total Yields Provided: 2 Servings

Ingredient List:
- Medium tomatoes (2)
- Red bell pepper (.5 of 1)
- English cucumber(.5 of 1)
- Medium avocado (.5 of 1)
- Fresh lime juice (2 tbsp.)
- Cilantro (2 tbsp.)
- Red onion (.75 tsp)
- Celtic sea salt (.25 tsp.)
- Red pepper flakes (2 pinches)
- Freshly cracked black pepper (.125 tsp.)
- Ice cubes (1 cup)

Ingredient List - Optional Boosters
- Olive oil (1 tbsp.)
- Finely chopped jalapeno chile (1 tsp.)
- Finely grated lime zest (.125 tsp.)

Preparation Technique:
1. Remove the pit and cube the avocado. Remove the seeds from the peppers.
2. Chop the veggies. Throw everything into your blender (including any boosters).
3. Pulse using the high setting for 30 seconds. Check the texture and pulse another 30 seconds if desired until smooth and creamy.

4. Tweak the cilantro, onion, pepper, and pepper flakes to taste.

Spinach-Powered Smoothie

Total Yields Provided: 2 Servings

Ingredient List:
- Unsweetened almond milk (2 cups)
- Fresh spinach (2 cups)
- Frozen banana (1)
- Frozen mixed berries (1 cup)
- Coconut oil (1 tbsp.)
- Cinnamon (.5 tsp.)
- Raw almond butter (2 tbsp.)

Preparation Technique:
1. Rinse the fruit and veggies.
2. Add the almond milk and spinach into the blender.
3. Blend in the remainder of the fixings and mix well before serving.

Wild Coconut Curry

Total Yields Provided: 2 Servings

Ingredient List:
- Raw coconut water or filtered water (1 cup)
- Full-fat canned coconut milk (1 cup)
- Probiotic powder (optional (.5 tsp.)
- Dandelion greens (.5 cup)
- Avocado (.25 of 1 medium)
- Lime zest (.5 tsp.)
- Fresh lime juice (1 tbsp.)
- Yellow curry powder (.5 tsp.)
- Red pepper flakes (.125 tsp.)
- Celtic sea salt (1 pinch)
- Frozen mango (2 cups)

Optional Boosters:
- Coconut oil (in liquid form (1 tbsp.)
- Goji powder (1 tbsp.)
- Ground turmeric (.125 tsp.)

Preparation Technique:
1. Remove the pit and peel the avocado. Finely grate the lime and squeeze for the juice.
2. Add each of the fixings into your blender (including any boosters).
3. Prepare using the high setting for about 30 to 60 seconds until it's like you like it.

Chapter 5: Snacks

Dips & Spreads

<u>Alfredo Pasta Sauce - Vegan</u>

Total Yields Provided: Varies

Ingredient List:
- Medium cauliflower (1)
- Avocado oil (1 tbsp.)
- Coconut oil (1-2 tbsp.)
- Cashews (.25 cup)
- Cloves of garlic (3)

- Pine nuts (2 tsp.)
- Almond milk (2.5 cups)
- Yeast-free - MSG-free vegetable stock (1 cube)
- Fresh oregano & basil (1 small handful of each) or Dried (.5 tsp.)
- Himalayan salt & black pepper to taste
- Juice of a lemon (.5 of 1)

Preparation Technique:
1. Soak the cashews soaking in warm water to make them easier to blend.
2. Roughly chop the cauliflower, mince the garlic and toss it into a pan using the oil and pine nuts. Cook for 2 to 3 minutes.
3. Pour in the almond milk and the stock cube. Bring the pot to a simmer.
4. Drain the cashews, rinse and add to the pan.
5. Simmer everything together for 6-8 minutes.
6. Toss everything into a high-speed blender and add the lemon juice, herbs, salt, and pepper.
7. It's smooth, so you're ready to go!
8. Use this with zucchini zoodles, gluten-free pasta, or any other veggie dish or salad.

Avocado Green Pea Spread

Total Yields Provided: Varies

Ingredient List:
- Green peas - fresh or frozen (2 cups)
- Avocado (1 small)
- Green onion or chives (3 tbsp.)
- Lime juice (2.5 tbsp.)
- Himalayan crystal salt or sea salt (.25 + .125 tsp.)
- Black pepper (.125 tsp.)
- Extra green onion or chives (for garnish)
- *Also Needed:* Food Processor with an S-blade

Preparation Technique:
1. Remove the pit and roughly chop the avocado.
2. Finely chop the onion or chives.
3. Mix the avocado, green peas, lime juice, green onion, black pepper, and salt in the food processor.
4. Process until well-combined. Store in the fridge until time to enjoy.

Black Bean Hummus

Total Yields Provided: Varies

Ingredient List:
- Canned black beans (1 cup)
- Fresh lemon juice (2 tsp.)
- Basil leaves (1 small handful)
- Clove of garlic (1 crushed)
- Sesame seeds (1 large pinch)
- Optional: Red chili (as desired)

Preparation Technique:
1. Rinse and drain the beans. Crush the garlic clove.
2. Toss in the beans, juice, basil, sesame seeds, and garlic into the food processor.
3. Pulse and adjust using water or a portion of tahini.

Other Delicious Snacks

Chocolate Chip Banana Bread

Total Yields Provided: 10-12 Servings

Ingredient List:
- Ground flaxseed (1 tbsp.)
- Warm water (2.5 tbsp.)
- Unsweetened almond milk (.75 cup)
- Mashed banana (1.5 cups)
- Melted coconut oil (3 tbsp.)
- Vanilla extract (1 tsp.)
- Liquid stevia (.5 tsp.)
- Baking powder (1 tbsp.)
- Ground cinnamon (.75 tsp.)
- Almond flour (1.5 cups)
- White rice flour (.75 cup)
- Tapioca starch (.25 cup)
- Old-fashioned oats (1 cup)
- Dairy-free chocolate chips (.5 cup)
- *Also Needed*: Regular-size loaf pan

Preparation Technique:
1. Warm up the oven to reach 350°Fahrenheit.
2. Grease a regular-sized loaf pan with cooking spray.
3. Whisk the flaxseed and water in a small bowl. Let it rest for 5 minutes.
4. Combine the bananas and milk in a large mixing container with the vanilla, oil, and stevia.
5. Stir until combined. Fold in the cinnamon, baking powder, and salt.

6. In another container, stir together the tapioca starch, almond flour, rice flour, and oats.
7. Combine everything and fold in the nuts, adding the chocolate chips last..
8. Pour the batter in the greased loaf pan.
9. Bake your bread for 1 hour to 1.25 hours until the center is set. Cool before slicing.

Chocolate Mousse - Vegan

Total Yields Provided: 6 Servings

Ingredient List:
- Soft tofu (14 oz.)
- Vegan 70% cacao - dark chocolate (6 oz.)
- Vanilla extract (1 tsp.)
- Maple syrup (3 tbsp.)
- Almond milk (4 tbsp.)
- *Also Needed:* Food Processor or blender

Preparation Technique:
1. Let the tofu become room temperature and drain well in towels.
2. Melt the chocolate in the microwave or double-boiler. Cool slightly.
3. Add all the fixings into a food processor. Blend until very smooth.
4. Chill for one hour (minimum).
5. Serve in individual glasses topped with a portion of fresh raspberries and cream.

Dried Orange Slices

Total Yields Provided: 15 Servings

Ingredient List:

- Seedless navel oranges (4)

Preparation Technique:

1. Slice (don't peel) the oranges and slice into thin pieces.
2. Set the temperature of the dehydrator to 135° Fahrenheit.
3. Place the slices onto the dehydrator sheets.
4. Let it work for approximately 10 hours.

Almond Joy Energy Balls – No-Bake

Total Yields Provided: 2 Dozen

Ingredient List:
- Almonds (2 cups)
- Dates (2 cups)
- Unsweetened cocoa powder (.25 cup)
- Sea salt (.25 tsp.)
- Unsweetened coconut flakes (.75 cup - reserve .5 cup for rolling)
- Vanilla extract (.5 tsp.)
- Unsweetened almond milk (1-2 tbsp.)

Preparation Technique:
1. Add .5 cup of coconut flakes into the food processor.
2. Pulse to break up flakes slightly (approx. one minute). Don't over-process. Transfer to a dish and place to the side for now.
3. Toss the dates into the processor and pulse until they have broken up to form a ball.
4. Break up the date ball and add in the almonds, sea salt, cocoa powder, and rest of the coconut flakes.
5. Pulse for several minutes, wiping down the sides as needed.
6. Pour in the vanilla extract and one tablespoon of milk. Process into a ball.
7. Remove the mixture from the food processor and roll into two dozen balls.
8. Roll each one in the coconut flakes.

9. Keep it in the refrigerator for best results and enjoy for several weeks, if it lasts that long!

Fresh Cherries - Nuts & Cream

Total Yields Provided: 4 Servings

Ingredient List:
- Alkaline water: For soaking
- Macadamia nuts (10 oz.)
- Fresh cherries (2 lb.)
- Almonds (2 oz.)
- Almond milk (2 cups)
- Vanilla powder (1 tbsp.)
- Stevia (1 tsp. or to taste)

Preparation Technique:
1. Soak the macadamia nuts and almonds for a minimum of twelve hours.
2. Prepare the soaked nuts together with the stevia, almond milk, and vanilla powder to a fine and smooth texture in a blender.
3. Store in the refrigerator for a minimum of three hours.
4. Serve with a portion of the fresh cherries.
5. *Tip*: For a bit of variety, you can also use red currants or passion fruit.

Ginger Cookie Bites

Total Yields Provided: 13-14 Cookies

Ingredient List:

- Almond butter (3 tbsp.)
- Macadamia nuts (.25 cup)
- Raw almonds (.25 cup)
- Rice malt syrup (2 tbsp.)
- Coconut oil (2 tbsp.)
- Medjool dates (pitted (4)
- Ground cardamom (1 tsp.)
- Cinnamon (2 tsp.)
- Ground ginger (3 tsp. or as desired for spice)
- Nutmeg (1 pinch)
- Oats (1 cup)

Preparation Technique:

1. Soak the dates in hot water for a few minutes before you start.
2. Blitz the soaked dates, syrup, almond butter, nutmeg, cardamom, cinnamon, ginger, and coconut oil in a food processor.
3. Add the rest of the fixings and blend until the batter is incorporated - but still chunky.
4. Roll the balls and flatten them.
5. Freeze for 30 minutes and transfer to the refrigerator to enjoy.

Pumpkin Bread - Gluten-Free

Total Yields Provided: 6-8 Servings

Ingredient List:
- Water (3.5 to 5 tbsp.)
- Pumpkin (1 small)
- Baking powder (2 tsp.)
- GF flour (2.5 cups)
- Italian seasoning (1 tsp.)
- Oil -Hemp or flax - etc. (2 tbsp.)

Preparation Technique:
1. Warm up the oven in advance to 392° Fahrenheit.
2. Arrange the entire pumpkin in a baking pan.
3. Bake for a minimum of 40 to 50 minutes. The pumpkin will become softened.
4. Cool for 30 minutes. Discard the skin, seeds, and stalk.
5. Mash the pumpkin well and combine with the remaining fixings.
6. Place the pumpkin onto a floured surface.
7. Knead until the mixture becomes sponge-like. If it's too sticky, just add a little more water.
8. Shape the mixture into a circular loaf shape. Arrange on a lightly oiled baking tray. Make a pattern in the top of the loaf, such as a cross.
9. Bake until done or for 30 to 40 minutes.

Quinoa & Hummus Wraps

Total Yields Provided: 4 Servings

Ingredient List:
- Cold water (2 cups)
- Quinoa (1 cup)
- Collard leaves (4 large or as needed)
- Sprouts (.5 cup)
- Carrots or Purple cabbage - shredded (.5 cup)
- Beetroot (.5 cup)
- Hummus (1 cup)
- Avocado (1 cup)

Preparation Technique:
1. Cook and mash or thinly slice the beetroot.
2. Pour the quinoa and cold water into a pan.
3. Simmer using the lowest heat setting until the quinoa is fluffy and the water is evaporated.
4. Prep the collard leaves. Rinse and lay them on the countertop like a regular wrap.
5. Prepare and scoop the fixings and quinoa between the leaves and then fill in with the remainder of the fixings.
6. Wrap by folding at the bottom and roll into a regular wrap shape.

Spiced Pear & Apple Crumble

Total Yields Provided: 2 Servings

Ingredient List:
- Coconut oil (1 tbsp.)
- Green apple (1)
- Pear (1)
- Cinnamon (1 tsp.)
- Nutmeg (.5 tsp.
- Gluten-free rolled oats (.25 cup)
- Chopped raw almonds (.25 cup)

Preparation Technique:
1. Use a sauté pan to heat the oil. Slice and add the apples and pears.
2. Sprinkle the mixture with the cinnamon and nutmeg.
3. Cook until the fruit is tender or about 5 minutes.
4. Spoon the fruit into the bowls.
5. Top with oats, almonds, and a touch of cinnamon.

Strawberry Sorbet

Total Yields Provided: 4-6 Servings

Ingredient List:

- Sliced strawberries (2.5 cups)
- Liquid stevia (4-6 drops)
- Thick coconut milk (.75 cup)

Preparation Technique:

1. Combine the coconut milk with the strawberries in a blender.
2. Use the high-speed setting until it's blended.
3. Add the stevia and blend until smooth.
4. Serve immediately or freeze it to thicken.

Stuffed Coconut Figs

Total Yields Provided: 10 Servings

Ingredient List:
- Dried figs (10)
- Ground/shredded coconut (.25 cup)
- Whole pecans (10)
- Raw almond butter (10 tsp.)

Preparation Technique:
1. Use a sharp knife to slice the figs to fill with the almond butter.
2. Roll the fig through the coconut and top with a pecan.
3. *Option 2*: You can also process in a food processor before rolling in the coconut.
4. Enjoy any time.

Zucchini Muffins

Total Yields Provided: 12 Servings

Ingredient List:
- Shredded zucchini (2 cups)
- Buckwheat flour (2.5 cups)
- White rice flour (2 cups)
- Baking powder (1 tbsp.)
- Baking soda (1 tbsp.)
- Ground cinnamon (.5 tsp.)
- Unsweetened almond milk (1.5 cups)
- Coconut sugar or brown sugar or stevia or maple syrup (.25 cup)
- Coconut oil (6 tbsp.)
- Bananas, peeled and mashed (3 medium)

Preparation Technique:
1. Spread your zucchini out on a clean towel then roll it up.
2. Wring out as much moisture from the zucchini as you can and then set it aside.
3. Warm up the oven to 355º Fahrenheit.
4. Prepare the muffin tins with liners.
5. Whisk the buckwheat flour, baking powder, rice flour, baking soda, and cinnamon.
6. Combine and blend the rest of the fixings except for the zucchini in a food processor. Add the dry ingredients.
7. Once the mixture is smooth and well combined, fold in your grated zucchini.

8. Spoon the muffin batter into your prepared pan.

9. Fill each muffin cup about ¾ full.

10. Bake for 18 to 20 minutes until done.

11. Cool your muffins for approximately five minutes in the pan. Arrange on a wire rack to cool the rest of the way.

Chapter 6: Dinner & Side Options

Broccoli Mushroom Rotini Casserole

Total Yields Provided: 6 Servings

Ingredient List - The Casserole:

- Whole wheat rotini - spirals or elbows (16 oz.)
- Broccoli (1 cup)
- Sliced mushrooms (8 oz.)
- Onion (1 medium)
- Large cloves of garlic (3)
- Dried basil (.5 tsp.)
- Panko breadcrumbs (.25 cup)
- Dried oregano (.5 tsp.)

Ingredient List - The Sauce:
- Almond milk (2 cups)
- Cashews (.25 tsp.)
- Clove of garlic (1 large)
- Nutritional yeast (.33 cup)
- Brown rice miso paste (5 tsp.)
- Smoked paprika (1 tsp.)
- Cornstarch (1 tbsp.)

Ingredient List - The Garnish:
- Paprika
- White pepper
- Herbamare or salt

Preparation Technique:
1. Warm the oven to reach 350° Fahrenheit.
2. Prepare a large pot of water with the salt.
3. Quarter and peel the onion.
4. Prepare the spirals or rotini for about 6 minutes just until al dente. (Don't overcook.)
5. Pulse the mushrooms, garlic, broccoli, and onions in a food processor. Toss into a sauté pan or wok.
6. Cook until softened (approx. 7 min.).
7. Pour in vegetable broth or water as needed.
8. Blend the sauce ingredients using a blender. Adjust the seasonings as desired.
9. Drain the rotini and toss into the pan. Add the sauce and toss to coat.

10. Prepare in a large casserole pan. Top with the panko breadcrumbs and smoked paprika.
11. Bake for 20 to 25 minutes. Enjoy when ready.

Butternut Squash With Spelt Pasta & Broccoli

Total Yields Provided: 4-6 Servings

Ingredient List:
- Olive oil (1 tbsp.)
- Spelt pasta (1 box)
- Butternut squash (1)
- Small onion (1)
- Vegetable broth (.5 to 1 cup)
- Basil, sage, or parsley (to your liking)
- Good-quality parmesan cheese (1 tbsp.)
- Salt and pepper (as desired)

Preparation Technique:
1. Warm up the oven to reach 375° Fahrenheit.
2. Prepare a baking tin with a layer of parchment paper or aluminum foil.
3. Cut the onion into quarters. Peel the squash and cut into 2-inch pieces.
4. Pour the oil into a skillet. Toss the onions and squash. Sprinkle using the pepper and salt. Roast for 30 to 40 minutes.
5. Cool slightly and pour into a food processor to puree. Slowly, add the stock until it's like you like it.
6. Prepare the pasta according to the manufacturer's directions.
7. Toss the florets of broccoli into the pot for about three minutes before the pasta is done.
8. Combine the pasta and squash sauce. Garnish as desired and serve.

Chickpea Frittata

Total Yields Provided: 2-4 Servings

Ingredient List:
- Sliced Broccoli/leftover veggies (2 cups)
- Scallions (to your liking)
- Garbanzo bean flour (.5 cup)
- Alkaline water (1.75 cups)
- Pepper & Salt (as desired)

Preparation Technique:
1. Pour a portion of oil into a skillet.
2. Sauté the broccoli or veggies of choice along with a few scallions until lightly cooked.
3. Pour a batter of the bean flour mixed with the water over the vegetables.
4. Cook until firm on the stovetop.
5. Use a sharp knife to slice the frittata into wedges and sprinkle to your liking with the pepper and salt.

__Crispy Cauliflower Buffalo Wings__

Total Yields Provided: 4 servings

Ingredient List:
- Water (1 cup)
- Cauliflower (1 head)
- Chickpea flour (1 cup)
- Garlic powder (1 tsp.)
- Finely ground Himalayan salt (.5 tsp.)

Preparation Technique:
1. Warm up the oven to reach 450° Fahrenheit.
2. Whisk or sift the flour, water, garlic powder, and salt until well incorporated.
3. Chop or snap the cauliflower into bite-sized pieces. Roll the cauliflower through the mixture.
4. Bake for 15 to 20 minutes. Shuffle around halfway through the cooking cycle.
5. Combine the hot sauce with the butter or oil in a pan to melt and stir.
6. After 15 minutes; transfer the cauliflower from the oven, and toss in with the sauce to coat each piece.
7. Roast for another 20 minutes until crispy.

Festive Holiday Slaw With Pomegranate - Salted Caramel Pecans & Starfruit

Total Yields Provided: 12-15 as a side/less for full servings

Ingredient List - The Pecans
- Olive oil (2 tbsp.)
- Lucuma powder - divided (4 tsp. + 1 tsp.)
- Stevia (6 drops)
- Fine Himalayan salt (.125 tsp.)
- Cinnamon (a dash)
- Maple syrup (1 tsp.)
- Pecan halves (2 cups raw)

Ingredient List - Ginger Lime Dressing:
- Lime juice (2 limes)
- Extra-virgin olive oil (.5 cup)
- Freshly grated ginger (1 tbsp.)
- Stevia (8-10 drops)
- Maple syrup (1 tbsp.)
- Salt & pepper (as desired)

Ingredient List - Slaw:
- Napa cabbage (1finely sliced)
- White cabbage (.25 of 1 - finely sliced)
- Finely chopped mint leaves (.5 cup + a few for garnish)
- Pomegranate (1 large - seeded)
- Star fruit (1 sliced)

Preparation Technique:
1. Soak the nuts to absorb the flavors.
2. Mix the oil and the 3 tsp. of lucuma. Whisk until smooth.
3. Add the stevia, salt, and cinnamon. Stir well.
4. Add 1 teaspoon of maple syrup and stir gently just to combine to thicken and become creamy - don't over-stir.
5. Fold in pecans, tossing well to coat. Sprinkle with the extra teaspoon of lucuma to dry the nuts out. Set them aside.
6. Prepare the dressing. Whisk each of the fixings and set aside
7. Shred the cabbage, chop the mint, and seed the pomegranate.
8. Combine all of these fixings in a large salad bowl, saving a portion of the pomegranate seeds to garnish.
9. Gently work in the pecans saving a few to sprinkle on the top of the dish before serving. Toss in the sliced star fruit, the pomegranate seeds, pecans, and a few more mint leaves.
10. Drizzle with the dressing and serve.

Garbanzo Zucchini Cakes

Total Yields Provided: 8 to 10 Cakes

Ingredient List:
- Garbanzo bean flour (.5 cup)
- Yellow onions (.25 cup)
- Green onions (.25 cup)
- Cayenne powder (.5 tsp.)
- Zucchini (2-3)
- Parsley (1 tsp.)
- Sea salt (1 tsp.)
- Onion powder (1 tsp.)
- Oregano (1 tsp.)
- Hemp milk (.25 cup)
- Grapeseed oil (as needed)
- *Also Needed*: Food Processor with Grater

Preparation Technique:
1. Chop the onions. Shred up the zucchini with a grater. Squeeze the moisture out of zucchini by hand using a strainer.
2. Mix the milk, zucchini, flour, onions, and seasonings.
3. Pour grapeseed oil to a skillet using the medium temperature setting to fry the mixture lightly.
4. Scoop the zucchini mixture and place in the skillet. Pat it down with the spatula.
5. Let the cake cool for about three to five minutes per side. Serve.

Ginger Creamed Pecans & Chopped Kale With Pomelo

Total Yields Provided: 1 large

Ingredient List:

- Pecans (.5 cup)**
- Extra-virgin olive oil (.25 cup)
- Fresh lemon juice (2 tbsp.)
- Filtered water (.25 cup)
- Freshly grated ginger (.5 tbsp.)
- Green onion, use the white parts mostly (1 tbsp.)
- Himalayan or Celtic salt (1 pinch)
- Stevia (8 drops) or optionally 4 drops or stevia + 1 tsp coconut nectar
- Kale (3 cups)
- Red cabbage (1 cup)
- Pomelo (.25 of 1)
- Radishes (2)
- Avocado (.5 of 1)

Preparation Technique:

1. Prepare the dressing.
2. Pour the water, olive oil, presoaked pecans, lemon juice, green onion, fresh ginger, salt, and stevia/coconut nectar into a blender. Process the mixture, scraping down the sides until a creamy mixture is reached. Pour into a serving dish and set aside.
3. Peel and remove the membranes from the pomelo. Slice the avocado. Chop the kale and finely sliced cabbage. Add to a salad bowl and toss gently.
4. Top with pecans, pomelo, avocado, and radish. Toss the dressing.
5. Enjoy or let it rest five minutes or so.

6. **Special Note:** It is best for the nuts to be soaked overnight, preferably or 30-60 minutes at the least.

Greens & Tomatoes With Sprouted Lentils

Total Yields Provided: 2-3 Servings

Ingredient List:
- Sprouted lentils (1 cup)
- Vegetable broth (3 cups)
- Shallot or white onion (.66 cup)
- Garlic cloves (6)
- Extra-virgin coconut oil (2 tbsp.)
- Diced tomato (2 cups)
- Freshly grated ginger (2 tsp.)
- Sun-dried tomatoes - packed in olive oil (8)
- Filtered water (6 tbsp.)
- Fresh spinach (4 cups)
- Baby kale (4 cups)
- Extra-virgin olive oil (spritz as needed)
- Fresh ground pepper & Himalayan salt (to your liking)

Preparation Technique:
1. Mince the garlic, onion, and sun-dried tomatoes. Dice the ginger and tomatoes. Chop the kale and spinach.
2. Cook the sprouted lentils with the vegetable broth.
3. Bring it to a boil. Place a lid on the pot and lower the temperature setting to low. Simmer until the water is mostly absorbed (20 min.). Extinguish the heat and leave covered.
4. Toss and sauté the garlic and onions in a saucepan using the medium-low temperature setting until the onions are translucent.

5. Stir in the fresh and sun-dried tomatoes, 2 tbsp. of water - heating only until bubbling.
6. Reduce to the low-temperature setting. Simmer to break down the tomatoes. Add the grated ginger and stir well.
7. Toss into the freshly chopped greens and add 2 more tbsp. of water.
8. Toss the greens into this mix and stir heating through for about one to two minutes. Stir in the cooked lentils.
9. Spoon onto serving plates and drizzle with olive oil. Dust with salt & pepper as desired.

Onion & Bell Pepper Masala

Total Yields Provided: 3 Servings

Ingredient List:

- Large onion (1)
- Bell pepper (1)
- Garlic cloves (2)
- Green chilis (2)
- Ginger (1-inch - grated)
- Cumin seeds (1 tsp.)
- Cashews (1 tbsp.)
- Asafoetida (.25 tsp.)
- Tomato ketchup (3 tbsp.)
- Red chili powder (1 tsp.)
- Garam masala powder (.5 tsp.)
- Turmeric powder (.5 tsp.)
- Salt (as desired)
- Vegetable oil (1.5 tbsp.)

Preparation Technique:

1. Prepare the veggies. Chop the chilies, cloves, bell pepper, and onion.
2. Warm the oil in a nonstick pan. Toss the cashews, asafoetida, cumin seeds, and turmeric powder.
3. Sauté until the cashews become light golden in color.
4. Toss the onion, ginger, garlic, salt, and green chilies. Sauté until onion becomes translucent (6-8 min.). Stir in the garam masala, ketchup, and red chili powder. Stir well.

5. Add the bell pepper, water for desired consistency, and salt to your liking.
6. Cook for about 5 minutes. Serve hot.

Pad Thai & Zucchini Noodles

Total Yields Provided: 6 Servings

Ingredient List:
- Zucchini (3 medium)
- Carrots (3 large)
- Chopped spring onions (1)
- Shredded red cabbage (1 cup)
- Bean sprouts (.5 of 1 pkg. or to your liking)
- Cauliflower florets (1 cup)
- Coriander/cilantro - fresh roughly chopped (1 bunch)
- Coconut oil

Ingredient List - The Sauce:
- Tahini (.25 cup)
- Almond butter (.25 cup)
- Tamari (.25 cup)
- Coconut sugar (1 tsp.)
- Lemon or lime juice (2 tbsp.)
- Clove garlic (1 minced)
- Ginger root (grated 1-inch)

Preparation Technique:
1. Use a sharp knife, a mandolin or spiralizer to prepare the carrot and courgette 'noodles.' Make the slices of zucchini and carrot very thin.
2. Toss the strips to a large bowl with the shredded cabbage, spring onions, rinsed bean sprouts, cauliflower, and coriander.

3. Prepare the sauce by mixing the almond butter, tahini, coconut sugar, tamari, garlic, juice of choice, and grated ginger. If it needs to be thinned, just add a small amount of water.
4. Combine all of the fixings until everything is covered.
5. Serve with a sprig of coriander and a spritz of lemon or lime.

Plant-Based Dinner Burger

Total Yields Provided: 8 Servings

Ingredient List:

- Red onion (.75 cup)
- Olive oil (1 tbsp.)
- Raw walnuts (.5 cup)
- Red quinoa (.66 cup uncooked/1 cup dry)
- Garbanzo beans - canned (1.5 cups)
- Tapioca starch - dissolved in alkaline water (3 tbsp.)
- Salt (.5 tsp.)
- Pepper (.25 tsp.)
- Smoked paprika (.5 tsp.)
- Sriracha - use ketchup for a less spicy version (1 tbsp.)
- Low-sodium tamari (1 tbsp.)
- Spelt buns
- Sweet potato fries
- *For the Topping*: Lettuce, red onion slices, ketchup, and tomato slices

Preparation Technique:

1. Prepare the quinoa according to the package instructions.
2. Chop the walnuts into small bits. Gently toast them using the medium-low temperature setting.
3. Drain the can of beans.
4. Warm up the oil and dice the onions. Sauté until softened and lightly browned.

5. Add to the food processor bowl; the toasted walnuts, garbanzo beans, onions, cooked quinoa, salt, pepper, smoked paprika, sriracha, tamari, and the tapioca starch mixture.
6. Pulse the fixings several times until the components are well blended - not pureed.
7. Prepare a baking sheet with a sheet of parchment paper.
8. Shape each burger by scooping .33 cup of the mixture to form a ball. Flatten it gently into a burger shape. Place the burgers on the baking sheet and chill them for at least 15 minutes before cooking.
9. Warm-up a few teaspoons of grapeseed oil in a frying pan for the crispiest burgers. Fry the burgers for about two minutes per side or until browned.
10. Serve on toasted spelt buns with lettuce, red onion slices, tomato, and ketchup. Sweet potato fries go great with these burgers.

Quinoa Stuffed Spaghetti Squash

Total Yields Provided: 2 Servings

Ingredient List:

- Spaghetti squash (1 large or 2 small)
- Coconut oil (2 tbsp.)
- Steamed green peas (1 cup)
- Shallot (1 medium)
- Orange or red bell pepper (1)
- Spring onions - white part (2 sliced)
- Chopped walnuts (.25 cup)
- Cooked quinoa (1.5 cups)
- Garlic powder (1 tsp.)
- Black pepper & Pink salt (as desired)
- Dried thyme (2 tsp.)

Preparation Technique:

1. Warm the oven to reach 400° Fahrenheit.
2. Wash and slice the squash in half. Remove the seeds and bake until tender (40 min.).
3. Heat half of the oil in a frying pan (1 tbsp.). Sauté the finely chopped shallot and bell pepper until softened.
4. Toss in the spices, cooked quinoa, green peas, and walnuts. Simmer until warmed throughout. Dust with the pink salt and pepper.
5. Divide between the squash. Put the fixings back into the oven for another five to eight minutes.
6. Transfer from the oven. Serve with fresh greens on top.
7. You can scratch the flesh with a fork, and it resembles spaghetti.

Quinoa With Asparagus - Beetroot - Avocado & Fresh Kelp

Total Yields Provided: 4 Servings

Ingredient List:
- Raw quinoa (1 cup)
- Boiling water (2 cups)
- Organic sea salt (1 tsp.)
- Fresh kelp (4 cups)
- Fresh green asparagus spears (4 cups)
- Raw beetroot (4 cups)
- Large ripe avocado (1)
- Fresh garlic (4 tsp.)
- Fresh ginger (4 tsp.)
- Fresh red chili (4 tsp.)
- Sesame seed oil (4 tbsp.)
- Raw seed mix (4 tbsp.)

Preparation Technique - The Quinoa:
1. Spiralize the beetroot. Roughly chop the asparagus. Finely chop the ginger, garlic, and seeded chili.
2. Prepare a saucepan of water and add the raw quinoa and sea salt. Once boiling, reduce to a simmer
3. Allow the quinoa to simmer for about 50 minutes or until it has absorbed all the water and appears fluffy.
4. Set aside to cool.

Preparation Technique - Assemble:

1. Chop the asparagus, garlic, ginger, and chili.
2. Using four separate serving bowls, place .5 cup of cooked quinoa in each bowl.
3. Top each bowl with the following:
    a. Fresh kale (1 cup)
    b. Fresh green asparagus (1 cup)
    c. Spiralized raw beetroot (1 cup)
    d. Garlic (1 tsp.)
    e. Ginger (1 tsp.)
    f. Chili (1 tsp.)
4. Divide the avocado into quarters. (Peel it and pit it.)
5. Slice ¼ of the avocado over the ingredients of each bowl.
6. Pour 1 tablespoon of sesame seed oil over each bowl.
7. Toss the ingredients and sprinkle 1 tablespoon of the raw seed mix over each bowl and serve.

Raw Veggie Chard Wrap With Ancho Chili Dip

Total Yields Provided: 2 Wraps/Dip (.5 cup)

Ingredient List:

- Filtered water (2 tbsp.)
- Raw almond butter (3 tbsp.)
- Fresh ginger (.75 tsp.)
- Fresh garlic (.75 tsp.)
- Dried ancho chili powder (.75 tsp.)
- Raw almond oil/Extra-virgin olive oil (2 tbsp.)
- Fresh lemon juice (1 tbsp.)
- Optional: Stevia (2-3 drops)
- For the Wrap:
- Avocado (.5 of 1)
- Large chard leaves (2)
- Cucumber (4-inch piece)
- Small red pepper (.5 of 1)
- Radish & Sunflower sprouts (your choice)

Preparation Technique:
1. Finely mince the garlic and ginger. Slice the cucumber into ten slender strips (lengthwise).
2. Mix the dip fixings (omitting the lemon juice), adding it last. Stir well and set aside for now.
3. Wash and pat dry the chard leaves and trim the stems. Arrange on a large plate and layer the veggie strips lengthwise down the center of the leaf. Roll and secure with a toothpick to hold it in place. Serve with the dip.

Spaghetti Squash Patties

Total Yields Provided: 2 Servings

Ingredient List:
- Spaghetti squash (1)
- Za'atar (.25 tsp.)
- Spring onion (1)
- Grated ginger (1 tbsp.)
- Coriander leaves (1 tbsp.)
- Ground flaxseed (1 tsp.)
- Oat flour - optional (2 tbsp.)
- Leeks (.25 cup)
- Coriander (1 tsp.)
- Sunflower oil (2 tbsp.)

Ingredient List - The Dressing:
- Lemon juice (1 lemon)
- Tahini (3 tbsp.)
- Water (5 tbsp.)
- Himalayan salt (1 pinch)

Preparation Technique:
1. Warm up the oven to 350° Fahrenheit.
2. Finely chop the leeks and coriander leaves. Cut the spaghetti squash in half (lengthways down the center). Discard the seeds and spritz with about half of the oil.
3. Bake for about 40 minutes.

1. Cool to the touch scoop out the insides with a fork, keeping the 'spaghetti' strands intact and toss into a bowl.
2. Add to the squash with the Za'atar, leeks, grated ginger, and ground flaxseed. Combine with the oat flour and chill in the fridge.
3. Prepare the dressing by adding all the fixings, whisking in a mason jar or a glass using a fork.
4. Warm up the remainder of the oil in a skillet. Make the patties and arrange them in the pan.
5. Sear until golden for about two minutes per side.
6. Serve with a portion of tahini dressing and a green salad.

Spinach & Rice Balls

Total Yields Provided: 12 Balls

Ingredient List Pt. 1:
- Spinach leaves (4.5 cups)
- Pitted Greek olives (.33 cup)
- Nutritional yeast (1 tbsp.)
- Garlic powder (1 tsp.)
- Salt (.75 tsp.)
- Lemon juice (1 tbsp.)

Ingredient List - Pt.2:
- Cooked rice (1.25 cups)
- Ground almonds (.5 cup)
- Chickpea flour (.5 cup)

Ingredient List - The Garnish:
- Cashew sour cream or coconut yogurt

Preparation Technique:
1. Warm the oven to reach 360° Fahrenheit. Prepare a baking tin with a layer of parchment baking paper.
2. Add all ingredients of part 1 into a food processor and mix well.
3. Dump into a mixing container and mix in the ingredients of part 2.
4. Mix well until you get a nice dough-like texture.
5. Create roughly 12 balls with your hands and arrange on the prepared baking tray.

6. Bake for approximately 20 to 25 minutes.
7. Serve using the cashew sour cream or coconut yogurt.

Stir-Fry With Lime & Coconut Quinoa

Total Yields Provided: 4 Servings

Ingredient List - The Quinoa:
- Quinoa (1.5 cups)
- Lime (1 zested)
- Full-fat coconut milk (15 oz. can)
- Water or vegetable broth (1 cup)

Ingredient List - The Sauce:
- Coconut aminos or Tamari - GF (.5 cup)
- Garlic (1 clove)
- Fresh ginger (1 tsp.)

Ingredient List - The Stir-Fry:
- Coconut oil (2 tbsp.)
- Garlic (2 cloves)
- Fresh ginger (2 tsp.)
- White onion (1 small)
- Celery stalk (1)
- Green beans or broccoli (1 cup)
- Baby bok choy (4)
- Snow peas (.5 cup)
- Cilantro (.5 of 1 bunch)

Preparation Technique:
1. Mince the ginger and garlic. Chop the bok choy, onion, cilantro, and celery.

2. Combine the lime zest, quinoa, broth, and coconut milk in a pot using the high-heat temperature setting. Once boiling, lower the setting to just simmering, and cover.
3. Simmer about 30 minutes until all of the liquid is absorbed in the quinoa.
4. Mix all of the fixings for the teriyaki sauce. Simmer until it's syrupy. Transfer the pan from the hot burner.
5. In a large pan with sides or a wok, heat the coconut oil.
6. Once it's hot, toss in the ginger, garlic, and onions. Sauté until browned, adding oil if needed.
7. Toss in all of your veggies except for the cilantro. Stir well and put a lid on the pan so the veggies can steam for 5 to 10 minutes.
8. Add a serving of quinoa into a bowl with the veggies, and a spoonful of teriyaki sauce. Top it off with the cilantro.

Stuffed Sweet Potato

Total Yields Provided: 4 Servings

Ingredient List:
- Medium-sized sweet potatoes (2)
- Red bell pepper (1 cubed)
- Broccoli florets (.66 cup)
- Parsley finely chopped (.33 cup)
- Clove of garlic (1)
- Caraway seeds (.25 tsp.)
- Melted coconut oil (2 tbsp.)
- Water (.25 cup)
- Lemon juice and zest (1)
- Fresh dill (.25 cup)
- Himalayan salt (1 pinch)
- Feta Cheese (.75 oz. - optional)

Preparation Technique:
1. Cut the pepper into cubes and the broccoli into florets. Finely chop the parsley. Juice and zest the lemon.
2. Heat up the oven to reach 350° Fahrenheit.
3. Drizzle the sweet potato with one tbsp. of the oil and a sprinkle of salt. Bake for 50 minutes.
4. Open the potato and scoop out the 'flesh' into a bowl. Try not to rip the outer layer.
5. Warm up the remainder of the oil with the grated garlic and caraway seeds. Sauté for 1 minute.

6. Add half of the water, broccoli florets, bell pepper, and parsley. Sauté for another two minutes.
7. Pour in the juice of the lemon and the flesh of the sweet potato. Mix together for two minutes.
8. Add the lemon zest, rest of the water, and chopped fresh dill. Sprinkle with the salt.
9. Stuff the loaded fixings back into the potato skins.
10. Top it off with a serving with a sprinkle of herbs, sprouts, herbs or feta.

Sweet Potato Veggie Biryani

Total Yields Provided: 4 Servings

Ingredient List:

- Oil (1 tbsp.)
- Cloves of garlic (2)
- Red pepper (1)
- Sweet potatoes (2)
- Onion (1)
- Cauliflower (.5 of 1)
- Paprika (1 tsp.)
- Cumin (2 tsp.)
- Turmeric (.5 tsp.)
- Ground ginger (1 tsp.)
- Coriander (2 tsp.)
- Cinnamon (.5 tsp.)
- Basmati rice (.75 cup)
- Vegetable stock (4 cups)
- Passata (1 container)
- Chickpeas (1 can - drained)
- Spinach leaves (2 large handfuls)
- Black pepper (to your liking)

Preparation Technique:

1. Warm the oven in advance to 400° Fahrenheit.
2. Chop the onions and garlic. Slice the red peppers.
3. Cut the cauliflower into small florets. Peel and dice the potatoes.

4. Empty the oil into a large ovenproof casserole dish. Put it into the oven for a few minutes to warm it up. Add the veggies and spices. Mix well to coat and roast for 10 minutes.
5. Combine the rice into the vegetables. Pour in the stock and add the seasoning.
6. Lower the oven temperature to 360° Fahrenheit.
7. Cover with a layer of foil.
8. Bake until the liquid has been absorbed (20 min.). The rice will be tender at that point.
9. Stir in the chickpeas, the passata, and spinach. Bake for an additional ten minutes.
10. Top it off with a portion of yogurt drizzled over the top if you wish before serving.

Tofu Chili Burger

Total Yields Provided: 4 Servings

Ingredient List:
- Firm tofu (2 cups)
- Green bell pepper (2 cups)
- Onions (.5 cup)
- Organic chili sauce (6 tsp.)
- Sea salt or organic salt (.5 tsp.)
- Olive oil (2 tsp.)
- Pepper (as desired)

Preparation Technique:
1. Chop the tofu, bell pepper, and the onions into small pieces.
2. Pour oil in a pan and stir-fry the onions and bell pepper for around five minutes. Fold in the tofu pieces. Stir-fry for another 15 minutes.
3. Pour in the chili sauce, salt, and pepper. Mix well.
4. Add water as needed.
5. Serve when ready.

Vegetable Pasta With Tomato-Pepper Sauce

Total Yields Provided: 4 Servings

Ingredient List:

- Vegetable or spelt pasta (2 cups)
- Tomatoes (1.5 cups)
- Small red bell pepper (1)
- Sun-dried tomatoes (.5 cup)
- Small zucchini (1)
- Garlic (2 cloves)
- Onion (1)
- Chili (1)
- Fresh basil leaves (5)
- Cold-pressed olive oil (2-3 tbsp.)
- Sea salt and pepper (as desired)

Preparation Technique:

1. Prepare the pasta (pkg. instructions).
2. Dice the bell pepper, tomatoes, and zucchini into cubes. Finely chop the garlic, onion, and the chili.
3. Warm the olive oil in a pan. When hot, add the onions, garlic, peppers, and chili.
4. Fry for a couple of minutes. Pour in the tomatoes and zucchini. Cook for approximately 5 to 10 minutes.
5. Dust with the basil, pepper, and salt.
6. Serve the pasta with sauce and other toppings as desired.

Wild Mushrooms & Spelt Pasta

Yields Provided: 4 Servings

Recipe Ingredients:

- Cauliflower florets (12 oz. or 4-5 cups)
- Raw cashews (.5 cup)
- Chopped garlic (2 cloves)
- Wild mushrooms (2 oz.)
- Fresh mushrooms (4 oz.)
- Spelt pasta (.75 lb.)
- Finely minced chives (.25 cup)
- Nutritional yeast (2 tbsp.)
- Lemon wedges
- Smoked paprika (2 tsp.)
- Black pepper (.5 tsp.)
- Sea salt (1 tsp.)
- Olive oil (or vegetable broth if oil-free (2 tbsp.

Instructions for Preparation:

1. Soak the cashews and mushrooms (individually) in alkaline water to soften (30 min.). Drain and rinse well. Slice them into small pieces.
2. Warm up half of the oil in a large skillet.
3. After it's hot, toss in the cauliflower. Stir-fry for three to five minutes.
4. Pour in the rest of the oil, pushing the cauliflower aside.
5. Toss in the mushrooms and sauté until they're reduced in size by half and combine with the cauliflower. Transfer from the burner and keep warm.

6. In a high-powered blender, add .5 cup of alkaline water, the drained cashews, smoked paprika, garlic, nutritional yeast, pepper, and salt. Whisk well until very creamy.
7. Empty the sauce over the cauliflower-mushroom mixture. Stir and cover until the pasta is ready.
8. Prepare the pasta in salted water. Combine and serve with a portion of chives and lemon wedges.

Delicious Sides

Baked Beans

Total Yields Provided: 1 Serving

Ingredient List:
- Organic butter beans (1 cup)
- White onion (.25 of 1)
- Garlic cloves (1)
- 100% organic tomato paste (2 tbsp.)
- Dry mustard powder (1 tsp.)
- Coconut oil (1 tsp.)
- Cherry tomatoes (.5 cup)
- Cracked pepper & Sea salt (as desired)
- Smoked paprika (.5 tsp.)
- Liquid stevia (1 drop)
- Fresh baby spinach (1 cup)
- Avocado (.25 cup)

Preparation Technique:
1. Wash and drain the beans
2. Warm up a frying pan with the oil using the low-medium heat setting.
3. Dice and sauté the garlic and onion until softened. Slice the tomatoes into halves. Fold in the cherry tomatoes, butter beans, and tomato paste.
4. Simmer for three minutes. Add all the seasonings, including the stevia and continue cooking for another three minutes.
5. Serve with spinach and sliced avocado.

Brussel Sprouts With Lemon & Pistachios

Total Yields Provided: 4 Servings

Ingredient List:
- Olive oil (2 tbsp.)
- Pistachios (.75 cup)
- Lemon (1)
- Large brussels sprouts (16)
- Salt and pepper (as desired)

Preparation Technique:
1. Prepare the sprouts. Remove the leaves from the core, remove the end, and peel the leaves off.
2. Juice and zest the lemon. Shell the pistachios.
3. Warm up the oil in a skillet using the med-high temperature setting. Saute the pistachios and lemon zest for 1 minute.
4. Fold in the Brussels leaves.
5. Toss until bright green but crispy (5 minutes).
6. Sprinkle using the salt and pepper to your liking with a spritz of the fresh lemon juice.

Cauliflower Fried Rice

Total Yields Provided: 4 Servings

Ingredient List:
- Cauliflower (1 large)
- Kale - any variety ex. Tuscan kale (.5 of 1 bunch)
- Coconut oil (1 tbsp.)
- Zucchini (1)
- Fresh root ginger (1-inch)
- Coriander (1 bunch)
- Fresh root turmeric (1-inch)
- Parsley (.5 of 1 bunch - any variety)
- Mint (1 bunch)
- Lime (1)
- Spring onions (4)
- Almonds (2 handfuls)
- Tamari - Soy sauce or Bragg Liquid Aminos (1 tbsp.)
- *Optional:*
- Green chili (1)
- Turmeric & Ginger (1 tsp. of each powdered)

Preparation Technique:
1. Prepare the cauliflower rice. Break the cauliflower up into small florets and toss into the blender or food processor. Pulse until it's rice-like. You can also grate it using a box grater.
2. Do the veggie prep. Thinly slice the kale, quarter and then thinly slice the zucchini, and roughly chop all of your herbs. Discard the mint and parsley stems but keep the coriander stems.

3. Prepare your ginger and turmeric by peeling them. Scrape the back of a spoon over the ginger/turmeric and grate them into a large pan with the coconut oil.
4. Stir the coriander, mint, and parsley into the mix too, including the coriander stems.
5. After about 30 seconds, stir in the cauliflower and kale.
6. After another two to three minutes, add the spring onions and the rest of the herbs, and the tamari/Bragg.
7. Stir well and remove from the heat. Total cooking time for all of this so far should be under 5 minutes.
8. Roughly chop the almonds and stir in. Season to taste with lime juice if desired.

Cauliflower Mashed Potatoes

Total Yields Provided: 4 Servings

Ingredient List:
- Coconut oil (2 tsp.)
- Cloves garlic (3)
- Onion (1)
- Cauliflower (1 head)
- Carrot (1)
- Vegetable broth - yeast-free (.25 cup)
- Garlic powder (1 tsp.)
- Rosemary (2 tsp.)
- Parsley (2 tsp.)
- Black pepper & Sea salt - Redmond Real Salt or Himalayan (as desired)

Preparation Technique:
1. Chop the veggies.
2. Warm up the coconut oil in a large pot.
3. Toss in the garlic and onion. Sauté for about five minutes.
4. Fold in the carrots, cauliflower, and vegetable broth.
5. After it's boiling, reduce the temperature setting to low-medium.
6. Simmer for 10 minutes. Add more veggie broth if needed.
7. Combine and add the rosemary, garlic powder, salt, pepper, and parsley.
8. Use an immersion blender or a food processor to mash the cauliflower. Serve.

Chickpea & Spinach Medley

Total Yields Provided: 2 Servings

Ingredient List:
- Olive oil (3 tbsp.)
- Garlic (4 cloves)
- Onion - thinly sliced (1 large)
- Grated ginger (1 tbsp.)
- Grape tomatoes (.5 of a 1-pint container)
- Lemon (1 large)
- Crushed red pepper flakes (1 tsp.)
- Chickpeas - ex. Eden Organic (1 large can or as desired)
- Sea salt - ex. Himalayan - Celtic Grey (as desired)

Preparation Technique:
1. Pour the oil to a large skillet.
2. Rinse and drain the beans.
3. Dice and toss in the onion. Sauté approximately five minutes or until they start browning.
4. Zest and juice the lemon. Toss in the grated ginger, minced garlic, tomatoes, lemon zest, and red pepper flakes. Saute for about 3 to 4 minutes.
5. Fold in the chickpeas. Cook for another 3 to 4 minutes.
6. Toss in the spinach, and wait for it to wilt. Spritz with the lemon juice and sea salt.
7. Cook for an additional 2 minutes and serve.

Healthy Asparagus

Total Yields Provided: 1-2 Servings

Ingredient List:
- Asparagus (.5 to 1 bunch)
- Ground celery seed (.5 tsp)
- Ground clove (.5 tsp)
- Cinnamon (.25 tsp)
- Agave Syrup (.25 cup)
- Bragg's Liquid Amino (1 tbsp.)
- Cold-pressed oil ex. olive (.25 cup)
- Alkaline water (.25 cup)

Preparation Technique:
1. Wash the asparagus and cut away the ends. Place in a shallow dish.
2. Combine the rest of the fixings in a blender.
3. Cover with this mixture and chill in the fridge for about 24 hours.
4. Serve and enjoy as a side dish.

Roasted Root Vegetables

Total Yields Provided: 4 Servings

Ingredient List:
- Pumpkin seeds (.25 cup)
- A mixture of the following root vegetables: Parsnips, radishes, turnips, carrots, beets, sweet potatoes (1-2 lbs. total)
- Coconut oil (2 tbsp.)
- Sea salt - Celtic Grey or Himalayan (as desired)

Preparation Technique:
1. Warm the oven to reach 425° Fahrenheit.
2. Dice the veggies into small pieces.
3. Toss with the salt and coconut oil.
4. Roast until lightly browned in spots and tender (30 to 40 minutes).
5. Toss the pumpkin seeds with coconut oil and sea salt.
6. Roast with the vegetables for the last few minutes before serving.

Sesame Ginger & Shiitake Cauliflower Rice

Total Yields Provided: 4 Servings

Ingredient List:

- Cauliflower (1 large head)
- Toasted sesame oil (2 tbsp.)
- Grapeseed oil (2 tbsp.)
- Green chili - ribbed (1 small)
- Minced fresh ginger (2 tbsp.)
- Minced garlic cloves (4 tsp.)
- Green onions - white and green parts (6)
- Shiitake mushrooms (4 cups)
- Wheat-free tamari (2 tbsp.)
- Cilantro (1 bunch or to your liking)
- Fresh lime juice (2 tsp.)
- Celtic sea salt (.5 tsp.)

Preparation Technique:

1. Remove the seeds and mince the chili, mince the garlic and ginger, and finely chop the rest of the veggies.
2. Squeeze the lime for juice.
3. Prepare the cauliflower rice. Roughly chop the cauliflower into florets. Discard the leaves and the tough middle core. Throw the cauliflower pieces into a food processor fitted with the 'S' blade.
4. Pulse a few seconds until the cauliflower is the consistency of rice (5 to 6 cups of cauliflower "rice").
5. Pour the oil into a deep skillet or wok. Heat the oil using the med-high temperature setting.

6. Sauté the ginger, chili, green onions, garlic, and mushrooms with ¼ teaspoon of salt for about 5 minutes or until softened.
7. Throw in the cauliflower rice and tamari. Sauté for another 5 minutes or until softened.
8. Stir in the lime juice, cilantro, and remaining salt. Tweak the flavors to taste.

Summertime Coleslaw

Total Yields Provided: 1 serving

Ingredient List:
- Red cabbage (1 cup)
- Napa cabbage (1 cup)
- Red pepper thinly sliced (1)
- Carrots julienne sliced (1.5)
- Bok choy sliced (1 cup)
- Chives (1 small bunch)
- Raw sesame seeds and lightly toasted - if desired (1.5 tbsp.)

Ingredient List - The Dressing:
- Bragg's liquid amino (1 tbsp.)
- Extra-virgin olive oil (1 tbsp.)
- Celtic sea salt (as desired)
- Fresh lemon juice (.25 cup)
- Toasted sesame oil (.5 tbsp.)
- Grated ginger (1 tsp.)
- Sesame tahini - raw (1 tsp.)

Preparation Technique:
1. Finely slice the cabbage, peppers, bok choy (with some green parts and mostly white), and carrots. Chop the chives into 1-inch pieces.
2. Combine all of the veggies in a large bowl.
3. Whisk and pour the dressing fixings into a measuring cup.
4. Serve with the dressing over all these vegetables
5. Serve immediately.

Tasty Bread Options

Gluten-Free Bread

Total Yields Provided: 4-6 Servings

Ingredient List:
- Pumpkin seeds (.25 cup)
- Flax seeds (4 tbsp.)
- Sunflower seeds (.5 cup)
- Walnuts (.25 cup)
- Almonds (.25 cup)
- Oats (1 cup)
- Buckwheat or coconut flour (.5 cup)
- Chia seeds (3 tbsp.)
- Psyllium husks (4 tbsp.)
- Melted coconut oil (3 tbsp.)
- Almond butter (1 tbsp.)
- Water (1.75 cups)
- Coconut flakes (4 tbsp.)

Preparation Technique:
1. Prepare all of the fixings to make the thick dough mix. Let it stand for at least an hour, preferably 2 to 3 hours on your kitchen bench. If you're leaving it for a while, cover with a kitchen towel.
2. Once you're ready to cook, warm up the oven to 350° Fahrenheit.
3. While that's warming, transfer the mixture into a loaf tin. It won't rise, so feel free to fill it right to the top.
4. Put the pan in the middle of the oven for even browning.

5. Bake for 20 minutes.
6. Take the bread out of the tin. Flip it upside down before continuing to bake for another 20 minutes.
7. Once it's been in for 40 minutes in total, place it on the countertop to cool completely.
8. It will last around five to six days if kept in the refrigerator in an airtight container.
9. Tip: You can mix together any nuts/seeds to the volume of 1.25 cups. It doesn't have to be these specific nuts and seeds.

Spelt Alkaline Biscuits

Total Yields Provided: 3 Servings (6 biscuits)

Ingredient List:
- White spelt flour (1.5 cups)
- Chilled grapeseed or avocado oil (.25 cup)
- Springwater or Perrier water (7 tbsp.)
- Agave (1 tbsp.)
- Optional: Purple sea moss gel (1 tbsp.)
- Sea salt (1 tsp.)

Preparation Technique:
1. Sift or whisk the flour and sea salt.
2. Pour in all wet fixings. Stir until all are combined
3. Use your hand to finish combining the dough
4. Break apart the dough into six pieces to form biscuits or roll it out and use a cutter.
5. Lightly grease the cookware with grapeseed oil.
6. Bake at 350° Fahrenheit for 12-15 minutes.
7. Put under the broiler for the last one to two minutes to lightly brown if desired.
8. Remove them from the pan let them cool some. Serve warm with agave or jam.

Spelt Bread

Total Yields Provided: 1 Loaf

Ingredient List:

- Spelt flour (4 cups + .5 cup more for kneading)
- Sea salt - fine (1.5 tsp.)
- Agave nectar (1 tbsp.)
- Baking soda (1 tsp.)
- Avocado oil (3 tbsp.)
- Unsweetened almond milk (.5 cup)
- Alkaline water (.75 to 1 cup)
- *Also Needed*: 8x4x3-inch loaf pan & Parchment baking paper

Preparation Technique:

1. Set the oven temperature setting to 375° Fahrenheit.
2. Prepare the pan with parchment paper across the width of the pan and spritz the pan lightly with avocado oil.
3. Whisk the dry fixings in a large mixing container.
4. Add in the oil, almond milk, and .75 cup of the alkaline water.
5. Knead until well combined. The mixture should be somewhat soft but hold together. Add small amounts of water by the tablespoon if it's too stiff. If it's too dry, just add more flour by tablespoonful until the dough holds together.
6. Prepare a floured surface and roll the bread gently with flour.
7. Arrange the dough in the pan and pat it so that it is evenly distributed.
8. Slightly score the top of the loaf lengthwise using a sharp knife.
9. Bake the bread for 45 minutes.

10. Take it out of the oven and cool completely in the pan before slicing.
11. Spelt bread is best served toasted, which crisps the bread and makes it even tastier.
12. Top it off with avocado sprinkled with lemon and smoked paprika.

Vegan: Spicy Sriracha Buttermilk Biscuits

Total Yields Provided: 4-6 Servings

Ingredient List - Butter:
- Vegan butter* (1.75 sticks)
- Salt (.25 tsp.)
- Asian Sriracha seasoning blend (1-2 tbsp.)

Ingredient List - Biscuits:
- Baking soda (1 tsp.)
- All-purpose flour (4 cups + more for dusting)
- Baking powder (1.5 tbsp.)
- Salt (1 tsp.)
- Compound butter (sticks from above)
- Cold non-dairy milk (1.5 cups)

Preparation Technique:
1. Take the butter out of the refrigerator until it's at room temperature. Dice it into cubes. Mix in the Sriracha seasoning and salt.
2. Add to a layer of parchment or wax paper. Work and form it into a cylindrical log. Place in the fridge to get cold or freeze.
3. When ready to prepare, just slice. Push in the pats of butter.

Preparation Technique - For the Biscuits:
1. Warm up the oven to reach 400° Fahrenheit.
2. Position the racks in the upper and lower thirds.
3. Prepare a baking pan with a layer of parchment paper.

4. Whisk the baking soda with the baking powder, flour, and salt.
5. Fold in the compound butter. Loosely toss until coated. Use your hands or a pastry blender to cut the butter with the flour mixture until it is the pea-sized.
6. Pour in the milk. Stir with a wooden spoon to form a shaggy dough.
7. Put the dough on a floured surface. Knead until it comes together.
8. Softly press out the dough to desired thickness.
9. Shape the biscuits and form with a biscuit cutter. Combine the scraps until all the dough is used.
10. Arrange the biscuits on the tray, almost touching.
11. Bake for approximately 20 minutes.
12. Cool for a couple of minutes to slice for sandwiches or serve warm with butter, or jam.
13. *Note*: To ensure that your biscuits are light and fluffy, it's recommended to freeze the butter; then grate it into the flour mixture.

Chapter 7: 21-Day Meal Plan

Enjoy each of these meal suggestions. You have the recipes for each one listed in the previous chapters.

Day 1:

Breakfast: Quick & Easy Quinoa & Apple Breakfast

Lunch: Curried Sweet Potato Soup

Dinner: Garbanzo Zucchini Cakes

Snacks or Dessert: Pineapple Green Smoothie

Day 2:

Breakfast: Avocado Wrap

Lunch: Roasted Sweet Potato Salad

Dinner: Chickpea Frittata

Snacks or Dessert: Chocolate Chip Banana Bread

Day 3:

Breakfast: Red Apple Pancakes

Lunch: Tomato & Black Bean Soup

Dinner: Spaghetti Squash Patties

Snacks or Dessert: Crunch Berry Smoothie

Day 4:

Breakfast: Maple Millet Porridge

Lunch: Cucumber & Tempeh Salad

Dinner: Pad Thai & Zucchini Noodles

Snacks or Dessert: Fresh Cherries - Nuts & Cream

Day 5:

Breakfast: Low-Carb Grain-Free Cereal

Lunch: Ginger & Asparagus Broth

Dinner: Tofu Chili Burger

Snacks or Dessert: Wild Coconut Curry

Day 6:

Breakfast: French Toast

Lunch: Zesty Alkaline Salad Brussels & Kale

Dinner: Plant-Based Dinner Burger

Snacks or Dessert: Pumpkin Bread - Gluten-Free

Day 7:

Breakfast: Buckwheat Crepes

Lunch: Thai Green Vegetable Curry

Dinner: Festive Holiday Slaw with Pomegranate, Salted Caramel Pecans & Starfruit

Snacks or Dessert: Mango Express Smoothies

Day 8:

Breakfast: Apple Cinnamon Quinoa

Lunch: Lentil & Beet Salad

Dinner: Onion & Bell Pepper Masala

Snacks or Dessert: Almond Joy Energy Balls – No-Bake

Day 9:

Breakfast: Super-Seed Spelt Pancakes

Lunch: Black Bean Chili

Dinner: Stir-Fry With Lime & Coconut Quinoa

Snacks or Dessert: Grapefruit & Green Tea Smoothie

Day 10:

Breakfast: Foolproof Weight Loss Breakfast Oats

Lunch: Kale Caesar Salad

Dinner: Wild Mushrooms & Spelt Pasta

Snacks or Dessert: Ginger Cookie Bites

Day 11:

Breakfast: Warming Blueberry Porridge

Lunch: Potato & Chickpea Curry

Dinner: Raw Veggie Chard Wrap With Ancho Chili Dip

Snacks or Dessert: Almond & Avocado Green Smoothie

Day 12:

Breakfast: Raisin Millet Breakfast Treat

Lunch: Spanish Bean Salad

Dinner: Spinach & Rice Balls & Healthy Asparagus

Snacks or Dessert: Spiced Pear & Apple Crumble

Day 13:

Breakfast: Chia Seed Fruit Overnight Pudding

Lunch: Broccoli - Mint & Ginger Soup

Dinner: Sweet Potato Veggie Biryani

Snacks or Dessert: Spicy Gazpacho Grab Smoothies

Day 14:

Breakfast: Mushroom & Bell Pepper Omelet

Lunch: Apple & Avocado Sesame Salad

Dinner: Broccoli Mushroom Rotini Casserole

Snacks or Dessert: Orange & Almond Cake With Vanilla Cream

Day 15:

Breakfast: Blueberry Spelt Pancake

Lunch: Carrot - Apple & Ginger Soup

Dinner: Greens & Tomatoes With Sprouted Lentils

Snacks or Dessert: Banana Smoothie

Day 16:

Breakfast: Easy Quinoa Porridge

Lunch: Detox Super Salad

Dinner: Ginger Creamed Pecans & Chopped Kale w/ Pomelo

Snacks or Dessert: Quinoa & Hummus Wraps

Day 17:

Breakfast: Pepper Avocado Quinoa

Lunch: Lentil Turmeric Soup

Dinner: Stuffed Sweet Potato

Snacks or Dessert: Spinach-Powered Smoothie

Day 18:

Breakfast: Vanilla Quinoa Porridge - Chai-Infused

Lunch: Brussel Sprout & Almond Salad

Dinner: Quinoa Stuffed Spaghetti Squash

Snacks or Dessert: Banana Cacao Smoothie

Day 19:

Breakfast: Pumpkin & Buckwheat Pancakes

Lunch: Vegetable Soup

Dinner: Crispy Cauliflower Buffalo Wings & Baked Beans

Snacks or Dessert: Cocoa Smoothie

Day 20:

Breakfast: Spelt Porridge

Lunch: Mushroom Wrap

Dinner: Quinoa With Asparagus - Beetroot - Avocado & Fresh Kelp

Snacks or Dessert: Banana Milkshake

Day 21:

Breakfast: Sprouted Toast With Cherry Tomatoes & Avocado

Lunch: Cauliflower & Leek Soup

Dinner: Butternut Squash With Spelt Pasta & Broccoli

Snacks or Dessert: Mint Chocolate Ice Cream Smoothie

Now, you see how easy working the vegan alkaline diet plan can be with proper planning. Keep up the good work!

Chapter 8: A Final Word

By now, you should have a good understanding of how to make better choices. There is one factor that is tied to your pH balance, and that is *your choices*. Your life revolves around longevity, your health, and even the propensity for disease. The following are some reminders of how to make better choices on the diet program.

Start every meal by loading your plate with servings of healthy plant-based food choices. Enjoy plenty of veggies to exchange the refined carbs. For example, select carrots or spiralized zucchini versus spaghetti. Exchange the white rice for or finely chopped cauliflower.

Forget that serving of cow's milk trumpeted by Grandma. Go for almond or soy milk. The same logic goes for those tempting fries or rolls. Choose yeast-free bread or wild rice.

Have a cup of alkaline broth. It's not only packed with minerals and vitamins; it's simple to prepare a veggie broth. Create meals around veggies versus a platter of starches.

Have a quick snack of grilled fruit or veggies and a healthy dip and forget those prepackaged alternatives.

Be aware of hidden acids lurking in sauces, condiments, and dressings. Choose to prepare your foods with cold-pressed olive oil and trash the butter or saturated fats.

Practice some relaxation techniques or a leisurely 30-minute stroll around the garden instead of enveloping yourself on the couch with a movie marathon. Above all, eliminate stress!

Attempt to drink at least 64 ounces of mineral water daily. Exchange alcoholic beverages for sparkling water.

Alkaline Supplements

You may not need all of these supplements, but with the growing amount of research involved around the alkaline diet, many recommend the additional benefit with the use of them. You should seek medical advice at any time you are unsure of the results you are achieving using the new aids and dieting plan.

Alkaline Minerals/Alkaline Salts: A high-quality alkaline mineral supplement is beneficial to help support your body. For example, the <u>pH Miracle's pHour Salts</u> essential alkaline minerals come in a bicarbonate form.

Potassium Citrate: You should attempt to take 99 mg daily.

Fiber: It is recommended to use psyllium husks if you are just starting out on the diet plan.

Calcium: For most adults, you should receive 1000mg daily. Calcium will help to reduce the effects of acidosis, which can also include decreased bone mineralization as well as hypertension. Always remember to keep the balance of calcium with vitamin D3 and vitamin K2, as well as magnesium.

Green Drinks: Enjoy these as a core supplement of the alkaline diet: a broad range of green vegetables, powdered grasses, sprouts, fruits, and more. You get a huge alkaline boost. Two to four times daily, have one liter of water with one scoop. For example, try Tony Robbins' Inner Balance Pure Energy Greens.

Omega Oils: Nuts and oils are the main sources, but you may need more than supplied by those foods.

Broad Multivitamin Or Mineral Supplement: Take one daily since everyone will have slip-ups and could be somehow missed.

Vitamin D: The usage of Vitamin D aids in the uptake of magnesium as well as calcium. It is suggested for you to consume 2000IU daily.

Conclusion

I hope you are now better informed of how to proceed with your dieting plan using your new copy of the *Vegan Meal prep: Plant-Based Diet Guide for a Healthy Permanent Fat Loss, Understanding Alkaline pH + Over 101 Whole Foods, Anti-Inflammatory Ready-To-Go Delicious Recipes Cookbook & 21-Day Meal Plan.* I also hope it was informative and provided you with all of the tools you need to achieve your goals - whatever they may be.

The meal plan is devised for flexibility. You can choose from any of the delicious meals to remain within the safe zones and feel much better as a result. The next step is to head to the superstore and get all the goodies you want for your first meal. You can always alternate it with another one of the delicious options offered throughout your new cookbook.

A Few Final Tips:

1. Get more exercise. Try taking a walk in the fresh air daily. It is a great alkaliser because it will get your lymph system moving.

2. Enjoy a large, raw green salad daily if possible.

3. Cleanse your liver with a highly alkalizing, freshly squeezed lemon juice in warm water first thing in the morning.

4. Reduce your intake of prepackaged foods as well as refined oils and alcohol. These are foods that cause an over-acidity in your body

Finally, if you found this book useful in any way, a review on Amazon is always appreciated!

- For us, people's health is fundamental, which is why we decided to create this essential guide. We hope with all our heart that you enjoyed it and we hope you can recommend it to your friends or loved ones -

Because being healthy is everyone's right.

THANK YOU

Copyright © 2019 Aqiyl Moore
All rights reserved.

Made in the USA
Coppell, TX
27 December 2019